Kata

**For the Transmission
of High-Level
Combative
Skills**

Vol. 2

An
Anthology
of Articles
from the
*Journal of
Asian Martial Arts*

Edited by Michael A. DeMarco, M.A.

Copyright © 2015 by
Via Media Publishing Company
941 Calle Mejia #822
Santa Fe, NM 87501 USA
E-mail: md@goviamedia.com

All articles in this anthology were originally published in the *Journal of Asian Martial Arts*.
Listed according to the table of contents for this anthology:

Book and cover design by Via Media Publishing Company
Edited by Michael A. DeMarco, M.A.

ISBN: 978-1-893765-14-6

Cover illustration
Painting courtesy of Feodor Tamarsky.
Copyright by F. Tamarsky. www.tamarskygallery.com

contents

CHAPTERS

preface

We all know the meaning of the word kata. Even to nonpractitioners it is a familiar karate practice. Plus, the word has long been incorporated into the English language. For this reason I choose to write the plural as "katas," and not follow the Japanese tradition where "kata" can be both singular or plural. By doing this I've ruffled feathers already, since many hold such a sacred bond with the time and place where karate took shape. Trouble with one word? Now how about the whole Okinawan martial tradition as passed on through katas?

A kata is much like a family jewel that has passed down through generations. It holds a significance that is difficult to decipher, and many dispute the meaning of every micromovement it contains. Who created it? What are the applications? Is kata practice outdated? Is there more than we can see and understand? You bet.

It is precisely because of the confusion and misunderstandings regarding the place of kata in the karate tradition that we are thrilled to present a two-volume e-book on this subject. If katas are learning tools that pass down knowledge of a valued art, then the authors included in this anthology can certainly facilitate the learning process for all interested in karate. Each author has excellent experience in the field, having studied directly under masters, often on the largest island in the Ryukyu island chain. In addition to their long years of physical participation in the school of hard knocks, their depth of scholarly research into the encompassing culture allows their writings to illuminate many aspects of kata practice that normally go unnoticed.

In our quest to better understand the full significance of kata practice, we must take a serious look at why old masters formulated the routines. How can kata practice better our health and promise to hone our self-defense skills? Each chapter in this anthology deals with the principles that guide kata practice. Hopefully the reading will reveal some of the secrets to improving techniques. As with other martial traditions, some insights cannot be shared through written word. Like good teachers, may the chapters here inspire you to look deeper into kata practice.

Michael A. DeMarco
Santa Fe
September 2015

author bio notes

Fernando Portela Câmara, M.D., is head of the Epidemiological Research Section of IM-UFRJ (University of Brazil). He holds a Ph.D. in biophysics with postdoctoral experience in data mining. A longtime practitioner and researcher of Okinawan martial arts, he began his training under Akamine Seiichi, a student of Izumikawa Kanki, and he is currently ranked seventh dan in Goju-Ryu. He runs the Shoreijikan, a small, private dojo in Rio de Janeiro, Brasil.

Perry Campbell, B.Sc., is a graduate of the geological engineering program at Cambrian College in northern Ontario and now works in the mining industry. Perry began studying karate in 1977 in Whitefish Falls, Ontario, under the tutelage of "the Yogi Man," Israel Segarra. He lived in Okinawa in 1990 and 1991, studying daily with Yagi Meitoku and Akamine Eisuke. He is a sixth dan under Senaha Shigetoshi and fourth dan, under the late Akamine Eisuke. Perry teaches a small group of students in his dojo, as well as conducting a limited number of seminars annually.

Michael A. DeMarco, M.A., received his degree from Seton Hall University's Asian Studies Department. In 1964 he began studies of Chinese-Indonesian kuntao-silat in the Willem Reeders tradition, primarily under Art Sikes, Thomas Pepperman, and Richard Lopez. Since 1973 he has focused on taijiquan: Yang style, Xiong Yanghe lineage; Chen style, Du Yuze lineage. He founded Via Media Publishing Company in 1991, producing the *Journal of Asian Martial Arts* and books. He teaches in Santa Fe, New Mexico.

Giles Hopkins, M.A., a teacher of English and history, received a B.A. degree in English literature from the State University of New York and an M.A. degree in history from the University of Massachusetts at Amherst. He has been training in the martial arts since 1973 and holds sixth dan rankings and a teacher's certificate in Okinawan Goju-Ryu and Matayoshi kobudo. His teacher is Kimo Wall, seventh dan and president of Kodokan, in the lineage of Higa Seiko and Matayoshi Shinpo.

Mario McKenna, M.S., holds a master of science from the University of Saskatchewan, and master of health administration from the University of British Columbia. He began his training in Okinawa Goju-Ryu and Tomarite (Gohakukai) karatedo in 1984 under Kinjo Yoshitaka. From 1994 to 2002 he resided in Japan, where he studied Ryukyu kobudo from Minowa Katsuhiko and Yoshimura Hiroshi, and Tou'on-Ryu karatedo from Kanzaki Shigekazu. He is ranked third dan, Gohakukai; fifth dan, Ryukyu kobudo; and fifth dan, Tou'on-Ryu. He teaches in Vancouver, Canada.

Notes

The Shape of Kata:
An Enigma of Pattern

by Giles Hopkins, M.A.

All photos courtesy of Giles Hopkins.

It should be known that secret principles of Goju-Ryu exist in the kata.

– Miyagi Chojun, founder of Goju-Ryu

Introduction

Kata has come to characterize karate in the popular imagination much as the *hakama* (skirt-like pant) calls to mind aikido or the slow-motion postures of an old man with raised arms might suggest taijiquan. Certainly there is more to karate than kata—supplementary exercises, strength training, using implements such as the gripping jars (*nigirigame*) or striking post (*makiwara*), prearranged (*yakusoku*) and free-sparring (*jiu kumite*)—but kata is the essence of karate. Katas contain the techniques and the principles of the art. Although in most cases the techniques may seem obvious to anyone watching a kata performance, there is still the question of how one goes about discovering the "secret principles" contained within the kata.

In a short article on karate and Japanese calligraphy, senior Shorin-Ryu teacher George Donahue recalled a conversation he had with one of his teachers, Nakamura Seigi, who suggested that there was nothing really hidden within a kata. Everything was there for all to see if they were "willing to use their eyes in an unfettered manner." While this may certainly be true, what, one might still ask, was Miyagi Chojun referring to when he mentioned "secret principles?" Is there more to kata than meets the eye or is this simply a question of semantics? How can something remain a secret if nothing is hidden? Nakamura, Donahue says, "preferred to call the 'hidden' moves 'intermediary' moves, because they occur between the obvious-to-the-eye basic moves" (Donahue, 2003).

Explanations are often quite cryptic in the martial arts, and this would seem to be no exception. There would seem to be nothing between the end of one kata technique to the beginning of the next. The kata is nothing more than a collection of techniques that have been put together in a pattern of movement. But it is this pattern or shape that is distinctive and makes the whole—the collection of individual techniques—greater than the sum of its parts. It is the pattern that contains the "intermediary" moves. So it is through a careful examination of the pattern or shape of a kata that one can discover the "secret principles" of the art.

The classical Goju-Ryu katas—what have generally been regarded as those katas brought to Okinawa from China[1]—do not conform to set patterns in the same way that the Gekisai or Fukyu katas, both katas of more modern origin, do. Modern katas like Gekisai I and II, and the Pinan katas of Shorin-Ryu, were constructed along specific and easily diagrammatical lines of movement, as if the patterns themselves preceded the techniques, almost like pounding a square peg into a round hole. The shapes of these modern katas have been said to resemble a capital "I" or an "H" or an "X." On the other hand, the classical Goju-Ryu katas seem to evidence a more organic kind of growth.[2] One indication of this is that these older katas are never completely balanced between techniques executed on the right and the left sides. This lack of symmetry has led to some interesting speculation about the age and origins of the classical Goju-Ryu katas, but much of this research is just that, no more than speculation (Swift, 2002). For practical purposes, it is sufficient to note that all of the classical katas share this quality of asymmetry to some degree.

Consequently, even from the most casual observation of kata performance, one will note that none of the classical subjects begin and end at the same point on the training floor. It would be fair to assume from this that the kata's floor pattern (*embusen*) is an accidental outcome of the techniques that are being demonstrated, and that the kata pattern was never meant to teach balance of movement or symmetry in the application of techniques. While that explanation for kata practice may be at least partially true for the patterns of the more modern katas—what are often referred to as training subjects in Goju-Ryu—it is certainly not the case for the classical subjects.

This is not meant to suggest that kata pattern's are completely arbitrary and without meaning. On the contrary, the karate techniques would largely be lost without the patterns. In other words, the kata—and by inference the kata's pattern—must mean more than some have suggested, not simply an elaborate method for training "posture, stance, body geometry, leverage, independent action of the limbs... etc." (Johnson, 2000: 121). At the very least, without the present shapes of the katas, our understanding of the techniques contained within them would be different, suggesting that the patterns or shapes of the classical katas are not so much related to the solo performance of a kata as they are to the application and meaning of the techniques (*bunkai*). The irony is that though few would debate the importance of kata as an encyclopedic collection of techniques that serve to characterize a martial style, few if any would argue that the kata pattern is just as significant.

Two Views of Pattern

In fact, for most present-day karate practitioners, the pattern has no real significance. If it is discussed at all, it is usually given no more explanation than as a kind of choreography to illustrate what one does when faced with multiple attackers. In this scenario, one begins a kata in the ready position (*yoi*), facing the front or north, using compass directions. If the kata's first move is a turn to the left or west, then the standard explanation has been that one turns to defend against an attack from the side. To continue this scenario, when one turns to the rear (south), the kata is demonstrating how one should respond to an attack from behind. But the absurdity of this explanation of kata—the multiple attacker theory—is shown in any kata where one turns a full 270 degrees (one instance of this occurs in the Goju-Ryu kata Sepai). It is obviously ridiculous when one is being attacked from the right side, for example, to turn a full 270 degrees to the left—turning one's back on the opponent in the process—rather than 90 degrees to the right.

Ridiculous or not, if one examines the applications of kata technique practiced in most traditional schools, and even what is shown in any number of authoritative texts, one sees that this multiple-attacker scenario is what informs the way most interpret the techniques of their kata. It is, in fact, reinforced in some schools by the manner in which the kata applications are studied. The student first performs the solo kata. When that is completed, the same student once again begins the kata, but this time with four or five students, each attacking from the prescribed direction indicated by the student performing the kata in their midst. As the student turns to his or her left to execute the first move of the kata, the student standing on the west compass point attacks with the appropriate technique. After the student has dealt with this attacker and begins turning to the right, the corresponding student on the east compass point attacks. The scenario continues in this fashion until the entire kata is completed. But the kata pattern is really insignificant here. In each case, the student has turned to face the attacker, meeting the attack head-on. When the pattern of the kata is used in this manner, it is not teaching movement.

Those who don't subscribe to this theory of multiple attackers, however, still seem to offer no plausible explanation for the many turns and stepping angles or degree of asymmetrical movement shown in the classical katas. Their explanation, based on the direction of attack, argues that the kata pattern sets up an imaginary scenario in which one can learn to respond to an attack from any direction. Certainly there may be some logic to support this view. The "Ha Po"[3]—the classic Chinese poem that seemed to capture the essence of the martial arts for Goju-Ryu's founder, Miyagi Chojun—reminds us that "the eyes [should] see in four directions." But one does not need the peculiar patterns of movement evident in the classical katas to teach one how to respond to attacks from different directions. If this were the reason for the kata patterns, one would still be left with the perplexing question of why all kata patterns were not the same. At the very least, one would expect all katas would be balanced to show attacks from complimentary directions if they were meant merely to show the directions of attack. Limiting one's view of the kata patterns to this rather simplistic and not-so-entirely-satisfying explanation seems a bit myopic and, in the long run, misses at least one of the fundamental principles of Goju-Ryu: to step off the centerline or, put more colloquially, to get out of the way (Hopkins, 2002).

Indeed, one is left with the impression that whatever key there once may have been to unlock the mystery of kata, it has been lost. Even some of the most knowledgeable karate practitioners and researchers seem to be resigned to accept the mystery and see kata, in the final analysis, as an "enigma" (McCarthy, 2001).

The author with Gibo Seiki.
The "Ha Po" scroll is hanging
between them in the training hall.

Stepping Off-line

A solution to the kata mystery lies in the kata pattern or shape. The pattern of the classical Goju-Ryu katas are meant to illustrate how one should meet or receive (*uke*) the attack. The patterns do show the direction the attack is coming from, but not so that the defender can turn and face the attack, to move either directly into or away from the attack, as is the case in both the "multiple attacker" and the "directional" interpretation of katas. Rather the patterns show one how to step off-line, in most cases, to avoid the attack and then counter.

Consequently, if one's defensive position in relation to the attack is different, the interpretation and application of the techniques will also be different. That is, if the steps and turns in the pattern of a kata are meant to illustrate how a defender steps off-line, out of the line of attack, changing one's angular relationship to the on-coming attack, then how the various blocks and counter-attacks are applied against the attacker will also change. This is why one's understanding of a kata's pattern or shape is evidenced in the way one applies the kata techniques; and, conversely, one's misconceptions about the significance of a kata's pattern are also apparent even from the most cursory examination of how one interprets and applies its techniques.

The Lesson of the Eight Directions

The "Ha Po," which one will find in many traditional Okinawan training halls enshrined or displayed somewhere on the walls, also admonishes the student to "hear in eight directions." The eight directions that this refers to are the eight points of the compass: north, south, east, west, northeast, southeast, southwest, and northwest.[4] In a martial sense, the eight directions refer not to the directions of attack but to the directions of defense: that is, how one may move in response to an attack. For example, if one is attacked from the front, one may defend against this attack by moving in any of the eight directions. How one moves in response to the attack is determined by the force, the speed, the commitment of the attacker, whether it is a left or right attack, the balance of the attacker, and one's own balance. One will then respond to the attack by moving to the sides, stepping straight back, moving away at an angle, stepping in at an angle, or stepping directly forward. In martial arts training—and this is certainly true of any of the more traditional martial arts—one trains one's sensitivity or "listening skills," as the Chinese so poetically put it, to "hear" what the opponent is doing to respond appropriately. And there are various exercises that different schools have developed to facilitate this training. The point is that the necessity of developing this sensitivity—how one responds to an opponent's attack—is common to all traditional martial arts, but it has received much less attention in karate.

TECHNICAL SECTION

Since it is the first in the canon of Goju-Ryu classical subjects, the Saifa kata is the logical place to begin any study of Goju-Ryu movement and the lessons of the eight directions. Saifa illustrates forward angle movement and lateral movement, using the front stance (*zenkutsu dachi*), the parallel stance (*heiko dachi*), the cat stance (*nekoashi dachi*), and what is sometimes described as crane stance (*sagiashi dachi*). The front stance is shown in both forward angle movement—most obviously in the three opening steps—and lateral movement. But while some of these movements may be apparent from any rudimentary performance of the kata or even a basic diagram of the foot positions, other movements—particularly the lateral movements—will remain hidden unless one understands the lessons contained within the shape or pattern of the kata. It should be noted that stepping in kata is dynamic rather than static and the stances do not so easily conform to the rigid classification of names that are necessary for any description in print.

Sequence #1

The first illustration shows the final position of the kata's opening sequence (1A). It is important to begin here if one is to see the transitional move or intermediary technique. Prior to the forward-angle step, there is a shift into a right-foot-forward front stance, with the left hand blocking and the right hand opening at head level (1B). This is followed by a step forward along the northwest angle, the left hand coming up as the right hand is brought down and the knee raised (1C). Most texts that attempt to illustrate or teach kata movement will only include the positions shown in (1A–C). Without showing the transition or intermediary move seen in (1B), however, the application of this sequence is lost. In the application of these moves, one can see how the forward-angle step is used against an attack (1D–E).

Sequence #2

In this illustration (2A), the final position from the previous kicking sequence is shown: a right-foot-forward front stance and hammer-fist at knee level. Again, it is important to begin here if one is to see the transitional or intermediary technique. In the moves that follow the kicking sequence in the Saifa kata, lateral movement using the front stance is shown (2B–C). This kind of defensive movement is not readily apparent unless one examines the question of why the kata turns a full 180 degrees, from a north facing technique in a right-foot-forward front stance to a south facing technique in a left-foot-forward front stance. Again, the "multiple attacker" or "directional" explanation of kata is less than satisfying here. If one accepts either of these explanations, there is really no need to turn at all or illustrate kata in anything other than a straight line, since one has simply turned to face the attack head-on. But if the attacker is stepping in from the west compass direction with a left attack, then the 180-degree turn shows that the defender has side-stepped the attack, using lateral movement in front stance, and, in the process, established a 90-degree relationship to the attacker.

Consequently, this also changes the way one interprets the hand techniques. The right hand—the hand closest to the attacker—blocks the opponent's left attack, while the defender's left hand simultaneously attacks the opponent's head or neck (2D & 2E). In utilizing the movement shown within the kata pattern, the technique is both faster and more powerful since the entire body and the turning of the waist is employed. In the moves that follow, the opponent's head is brought down and attacked with a half-fist or crab-shell fist to the neck or throat. This is followed by a hammer-fist strike.

8

Sequence #3

The first illustration in this sequence shows the final kata position from the previous sequence (3A): a left-foot-forward front stance and hammer-fist attack. In the moves that follow this sequence in the Saifa kata, lateral movement in parallel stance is shown (3B–C). But just as in the previous sequence, the lateral movement is not apparent from the kata movement alone. One must apply the lessons contained within the shape of the kata to see that by drawing the right foot into parallel stance and redirecting one's attention from the rear (or south) to the original front (or north) of the kata, one's centerline has shifted in relationship to the attack from the west. In this move, similar to the opening sequence of the Sepai kata (Hopkins, 2001), the attacker is stepping in from the west compass point with a right attack (3D–E). The left open-hand blocks the opponent's right attack, as the right forearm and hammer-fist is brought down onto the back of the opponent's head or neck. This sequence is duplicated on the other side in response to a left attack, again from the west compass point. The final technique of this sequence—a right-hand grab and left punch, stepping into a right-foot-forward basic stance—I have not illustrated. It should be noted that this "finishing technique" is only shown once, tacked on to the second of these techniques. This is typical of classical katas.

9

Sequence #4

The first illustration in this sequence shows the final kata position from the previous sequence (4A): a right-foot-forward basic stance with a right hand grab and left punch. In the moves that follow this sequence in the Saifa kata, the final turning block (*mawashi uke*), lateral movement in cat stance is shown. From a rear (south) facing basic stance, the defender steps directly forward with the left foot, pivoting in a clockwise direction to the original front, into a right-foot-forward cat stance (4B–E). Again, though the interpretations of most schools suggest that the attack is from either the south or the north compass point, since one's attention and physical orientation would seem to suggest this, in any practical sense this interpretation isn't very satisfying and by implication suggests that there really is no message contained within the odd shapes and patterns of the kata. If, on the other hand, the attacker is stepping in from the west compass point with a right attack, this last move in the Saifa kata is demonstrating lateral movement, shifting into a cat stance. The left hand is blocking the opponent's right attack (4F), while the right hand is simultaneously brought around to attack the head (4G). Once the head is controlled, the defender pivots back towards the front (north), twisting the opponent's head and neck with the mawashi technique (4H–I). It will be noted that the kata finishes in a cat stance to imply that the knee (*hiza geri*) may be used in the final technique.

Conclusion

This is the lesson contained in the pattern or shape of kata. The classical Goju-Ryu katas illustrate how to utilize the various Goju-Ryu stances—front stance, basic stance, parallel stance, natural stance, horse stance, cat stance, cross-footed stance—to move in any of the eight directions in response to an attack. Ironically, in learning how to apply the lessons contained within the kata patterns, applying the lessons of the eight directions, we also learn how to apply the hand techniques. If we don't understand the lessons of the eight directions, then we will not understand how the hand techniques are meant to be applied. The key, then, to the understanding and practice of karate, it will be seen, is in the shape of the katas, in the stepping patterns. If one begins to understand what the feet are doing, then, as that old Chinese scholar has said, a journey of a thousand miles truly does begin with the first step.

Notes

[1] The open-hand (*kaishu*) katas: Saifa, Seiunchin, Shisochin, Sepai, Sanseiru, Sesan, Kururunfa, and Suparimpei.

[2] I will limit my discussion to the classical Goju-Ryu katas, though I believe these points are true of the classical katas of all Okinawan arts.

[3] The "Ha Po" (sometimes called the "Kenpo Hakku") is a poem from the *Bubishi*, a famous martial text reputedly from China and passed down to a number of early Okinawan karate masters. There are many translations and much has been written about its history, its significance in the development of Okinawan

11

karate, and the cryptic nature of some of its contents.

4 Dr. Yang Jwing-Ming (1996: 95) also mentions these eight directions—forward, backward, two sideways, and four diagonal—in discussing movements in White Crane gongfu and martial styles related to White Crane.

Bibliography

Alexander, G., & Penland, K. (Trans. & Eds.) (1993). *Bubishi: Martial art spirit.* Lake Worth, FL: Yamazato Publications.

Donahue, G. (2003, April 1). "Kata, bunkai & calligraphy." http://www.fightingarts.com/reading/article.php?id=154

Hopkins, G. (2002). The lost secrets of Goju-Ryu: What the kata shows. *Journal of Asian Martial Arts, 11*(4), 54–77.

Johnson, N. (2000). *Barefoot Zen: The Shaolin roots of kung fu and karate.* York Beach, ME: Samuel Weiser, Inc.

McCarthy, P. (2001, August 26). "Kata: The enigma of Uchinadi." http://www.fightingarts.com/forums/ubb/Forum10/HTML/000008.html

McCarthy, P. (Trans.) (1995). *The bible of karate: Bubishi.* Rutland, VT: Charles E. Tuttle Co.

McCarthy, P., & McCarthy, Y. (1999). *Ancient Okinawan martial arts: Koryu Uchinadi, Vol. 2.* Boston: Tuttle.

Swift, C. (2002). The kenpo of Kume village: Speculation on the original Nafadi. *Dragon Times, 23.*

Yang, J. (1996). *The essence of Shaolin white crane.* Boston: YMAA Publication Center.

Acknowledgment

Special thanks to Brian Conz, friend and training partner, for his assistance in demonstrating applications for this article. And, of course, a very special thanks to my teachers, Matayoshi Shinpo, Gibo Seki, and Kimo Wall.

The Teaching of Goju-Ryu Kata:
A Brief Look at Methodology and Practice

by Giles Hopkins, M.A.

As the author practices a Goju-Ryu technique from the Seiunchin kata,
his son Noah finds it a natural position to hold his teddybear.
All photos courtesy of Giles Hopkins.

Introduction

Kata (solo routine) training has become a kind of modern-day Gordian knot; no one seems to have the key to untangle its mysteries. Few seem able to agree on what it means or what it was originally meant to teach. And there are a host of credible explanations that seem to have fueled the debate.

From a historical standpoint, a number of researchers have pointed out that even the origins of various Goju-Ryu kata are open to question—some arguing that certain movements are clearly reminiscent of Five Ancestor Fist, others suggesting a link to White Crane, and still others arguing that some form of karate may have been practiced in Okinawa since the 14th century, for all intents and purposes an indigenous Okinawan martial art. This last theory suggests that a blending took place in the early 20th century when a number of Okinawan teachers independently journeyed to China in order to continue their training (Co, 1998; McCarthy, 1995; Swift, 2002).

The question of lineage only further compounds the problem: whose lineage might provide definitive answers about kata? Again, we run into awkward historical questions and a lack of documentation.[1]

Interestingly, some have tried to reconcile these differences of interpretation, side stepping the whole question of historical precedent or lineage, by suggesting that katas contain an almost infinite variety of techniques or different levels of meaning—beginner, intermediate, and advanced levels of kata applications (Heilman, 1997; Higaonna, 2004: 7). Marvin Labbate tries to make this point in discussing what he refers to as "advanced Goju-Ryu techniques" (Labbate, 2000). Still others, armed with an arsenal of Japanese terms, describe kata as if it were an onion and the different applications of its techniques merely layers of hidden meaning (Craig & Anderson, 2002). There are even those who see kata as a transcendent and magical experience—as if katas were more shamanistic ritual than practical self-defense; that is, one merely uses them to achieve, through ritualized movement, a kind of trance-like warrior state, similar to what one might find in aboriginal tribal gatherings, the movements conveying a kind of mystical understanding on a subconscious level. Given such diverse views on the matter, it's no wonder that some have even suggested that katas were made to be intentionally ambiguous.[2]

It is my contention, however, that the fundamental problem—what has really fed this seemingly endless debate over the solo kata and its applications—may have more to do with how karate has been traditionally taught than where it comes from or who our teacher's teacher happened to be. It is a question of method, not lineage or historical antecedent, and the method has changed very little over the years. In fact, the methodology of teaching karate has become ritualized as much as anything else in martial arts, to the point where principles have been replaced by repetition. It is the method of instruction that gets passed on in this case, not the knowledge. In the process, the kata becomes something else, no longer a repository of specific self-defense combinations and movement principles. When this happens, the lessons of the teaching aids or mnemonics contained within the katas are largely ignored or forgotten, affecting how we see the applications of each movement.

Pedigree and Pedagogy

The practice of kata has become an almost sacrosanct tradition in karate schools. Over the course of endless hours of kata practice students are told, "Every inch of movement has meaning." With this encouragement, the teacher only hopes that the student will bring life to the kata. The difficulty comes with the student's understanding of this advice and how one learns karate, for the most part through imitation and creative invention.

Most movement, particularly kata movement, is taught through imitation: "monkey see, monkey do." There is little discussion or verbal instruction of kata in traditional schools and perhaps even less in non-traditional schools. Toguchi Seikichi, the head of Shoreikan Goju-Ryu until his death in 1998, makes this clear in his description of training in the old days on Okinawa: "Both Higa and Miyagi were very strict and questions were not permitted during training" (Toguchi, 2001: 16).

Yagi Meitoku, the senior student to have trained under both Miyagi and Higa, said that training in those days involved long hours of conditioning drills, and only after a number of years would Miyagi even begin to teach kata to a student. Few of Miyagi's students, Yagi says, learned anything more than the "beginner's way, with no understanding of what they were learning." Yagi goes on to say that Master Miyagi "would very rarely give insights or meaning to the kata that he taught until the student showed mastery of the form through hard and consistent training," and few, according to Yagi, stayed long enough to learn anything beyond the rudiments of kata (Babladelis, 1989).

This is still true in most traditional Okinawan schools today. The beginning student simply stands in the back of the room and does his or her best to follow the other students. What little verbal instruction there may be is usually simple and rudimentary: posture, breathing, and stance, for example. Beyond this, of course, the beginning student needs a great deal of repetition. Anything more than this—a philosophical discussion of martial principles, for instance—would be lost on the beginner; he or she has no basis for understanding it. Additionally, one might also argue that this traditional model fits the teacher's natural wariness of beginners, who, for the most part, are not likely to stay long enough to learn what the teacher may really have to teach, to learn anything more than beginner's karate. In the process, the teacher does not give away the "secrets" (the applications, in this case) of the kata to students who are not ready for them. A further rationale is that the movements must be thoroughly ingrained before one learns how to apply them or the movements themselves will be compromised in an attempt to force their application. The teaching method provides a natural safeguard against either of these scenarios. At the same time, however, students are left with the impression that the kata is intentionally cryptic in order to foster the creative interpretation of martial techniques—that is, the applications.

Since the kata is learned through imitation and explanations are rarely given, one is left in most cases to discover meaning for oneself. Anthony Mirakian, a well-known Goju-Ryu teacher and early pioneer in bringing Meibukan Goju-Ryu to America, supports Toguchi's observation that "there was very little talking" in the traditional Okinawan dojo. Mirakian goes on to say that, "Generally, once a student was shown the kata, he was expected to correct the movements himself . . . the applications were left to the student's imagination and inquisitiveness" (Schoene, 2004).

The trouble is that this discovery method, while rich and imaginative—perhaps even personally rewarding—gives the impression that any interpretation of kata movement that seems to work is okay. In fact, this line of argument suggests there is no wrong or right, just different points of view. However, if there is not strict adherence to both the movements of the kata and the principles of the kata, then one is not exploring the methods of a particular art but rather assigning arbitrary explanations to one's own, sometimes idiosyncratic, movements.

And this is the problem. When students learn kata solely through imitation—rather than in conjunction with a thorough discussion of the martial principles involved and illustrated in the kata—then the movements may be preserved but their applications will be misunderstood. For example, the rhythm and pauses used to teach a kata become habitual in the student, obscuring application combinations and the natural flow of sequences. When the kata is taught, it is slowed down and the techniques are fragmented in order to see the movements more clearly. This fragmentation, however, affects how one sees the applications as well. This is one instance where the teaching methodology—necessary perhaps to instruct a beginner in the rudiments of a particular kata—interferes with a more realistic understanding of the kata's applications.

In his last book, on the "advanced techniques" of Goju-Ryu karate, Toguchi, in effect, suggests that he developed his modern training katas to bridge this gap between kata and its applications. (These are the modern Shoreikan katas: Fukyu, Gekisai, Gekiha, and Kakuho). Traditional methods of instruction—that is, imitation without asking any questions—did not satisfy the inquisitive nature of American GIs, and so Toguchi developed a series of basic katas and corresponding two-person drills (*bunkai kumite*) to show applications. He did this, he says, because he "could not speak English" and he believed "a two-person sequence of the kata would give clear answers to the questions posed by the Americans" (Toguchi, 2001: 32).

However, these modern training katas do not provide the keys to understand the movement and principles of the original classical katas of Chinese origin.[3] This is particularly true of the two-person sequences that Toguchi developed—their techniques being elementary and the principles of Toguchi's two-person application drills misleading with their straight-line movement. So, even though this did introduce a different methodology into the instruction of karate, it did nothing to explain the movement or techniques of the Goju-Ryu classical subjects. The techniques and patterns are fundamentally different.

This hand position from Sanseiru kata illustrates another of the mnemonic teaching aids contained within the Goju-Ryu katas. The left hand is placed at the elbow to show where the defender would be holding the attacker in this arm-bar technique.

The problem, as McCarthy sees it, is that "the formula once used to interpret its [kata] application principles has all but vanished" (26 August 2001). But it is not the formula that is the problem. The formula is fairly clear once one knows how to look at the kata. It is the methods we use to teach karate that have obscured the message, and the methods have been passed on from teacher to student, maintaining a venerable tradition that in some quasi-religious sense is meant to test the character of the student through long hours of unquestioning repetition. The teacher's methods are not questioned; the teacher has attained his or her own exalted rank through the very means that he or she is using to guide the student. The same understanding will somehow be conveyed to the dedicated student—like a flash of Zen enlightenment—only after years of training. The kata becomes a kind of koan for the karate student; he tests his understanding of the kata as he delves into more and more creative explanations for the applications of the individual moves.

This is the traditional approach to the study of kata. The checks and balances that a thorough understanding of martial principles would provide no longer seem to exist.[4] They have been eviscerated by rationalizations of multiple interpretations or the mystique of advanced levels of understanding. Or they have merely sunk under the burdensome weight and authority of different lineages. Certainly the discovery method is not without its benefits. It forces the student, Anthony Mirakian says, to become "highly observant, one of the most important factors in mastering karate" (Schoene, 2004).

Some Principles
Useful in the Analysis of Kata

- Move off the centerline. The stepping pattern of kata teaches this principle. Directional changes in kata show where the attack is coming from and how to step off the centerline in applying the technique. The step and entry technique should be executed in such a way that the attacker cannot attack a second time. This is shown in the kata.
- Katas are composed of combinations or sequences of techniques. Each sequence or series of techniques begins with a "block" and ends with the opponent on the ground or finished. To understand kata, look for the beginnings and the endings.
- Basic techniques that are not shown in specific application sequences are generally put at the beginning of kata and performed in a series of three techniques, as in Shisochin and Sesan, for example. If a technique is performed in response to both a left and a right attack, then the finishing technique of the sequence is often only tacked onto the second technique.
- The legs and arms are connected. Body rotation and stepping that naturally accompanies each technique generates power. There is no chambering of the attacking hand, as it has traditionally been understood.

- Stepping forward with a blocking move in kata implies that one already has control of the opponent. Look for the initial "block".
- Block the arms, but attack the head. Remember that the Japanese word "uke" means "receiving." Using the word "block" creates a rather restrictive and unnecessarily rigid view of these techniques in kata.
- Don't look at final positions to explain techniques. A kata is not static, but always in motion. The real explanation is in the movement—the weight shifting, stances, arm and leg motions—that leads from the previous posture to the final position of the technique one is attempting to explain.
- Movement within sequences should be continuous and uninterrupted. No gaps.

The question is whether this benefit outweighs the drawbacks, considerable as they are, that have led to a general disagreement about kata and its applications.

The way we teach affects our understanding. This is particularly true of those mnemonic teaching aids contained in the classical katas. To illustrate, I will try to show how a few of the techniques of the Goju-Ryu kata Seiunchin demonstrate the sort of confusion traditional teaching methods have inspired and led to the very misunderstandings they were meant to avoid—in some cases, obscuring aspects of the kata that would lead to a better understanding of the system as a whole.

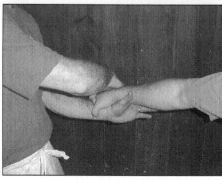

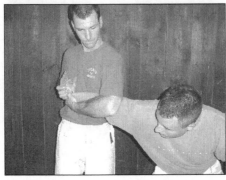

The position of the hands in this technique from the Saifa kata illustrates one of the mnemonic teaching aids contained in kata. The left hand is held around the right fist to show where the defender would be holding the attacker in this grab release technique.

TECHNICAL SECTION

Seiunchin is generally regarded as the second kata in the classical canon of Goju-Ryu subjects.[5] Each of the combinations within the kata deals with responses against an opponent's grab or push and shows the defender controlling the opponent as he counterattacks. Seiunchin contains six of these combinations, not counting repetition: four against wrist grabs and two against pushes or double-hand grabs. The variations—why there are two different responses to a push or double-hand grab and two responses against a cross-hand wrist grab, for example—counter differences in the attacker's strength and commitment to the attack.

It will be apparent almost immediately in some Goju-Ryu circles that it is highly contentious to describe the kata categorically as consisting of six combinations of techniques against very specific attacks. To suggest this is somehow blasphemous to those who see kata as a seemingly endless repository of technique.

The way we teach kata, in fact, seems to promote this encyclopedic view of kata. We teach a move at a time, not principles or applications. We dissect the movements so completely that the speed or rhythm we use in teaching becomes so thoroughly ingrained that it frustrates students who try to apply the techniques of the kata in the same manner that they learned them. This method of learning kata has two rather questionable outcomes: First, we tend to think that each small step or movement is a separate technique. Second, because the kata has been learned piecemeal, we fail to see that the gaps and pauses in movement inserted in places to facilitate learning are not dictated by the application of the various techniques. We tend to disconnect techniques that were meant to be a part of the same sequence. Erroneously, the rhythm and pauses used simply to teach the kata seem to suggest their own applications, or, since they are not recognized as part of the teaching methodology, they interrupt and obscure the kata's more natural application sequences.

Mistakes in Rhythm

Consider the opening moves of Seiunchin kata. The first move of the kata is a step forward, from the beginning ready stance, to the northeast (all directional references assume that the kata starts facing north) with the right foot, dropping into a right-foot-forward horse-riding stance (*shiko dachi*) (1A). The hands open and are brought in front of the body (1B). In some schools, the hands are open, palms facing, with the arms straight, perpendicular to the ground. In other schools, the arms are brought out towards the knees more, with the backs of the hands facing forward. In either case, however, there is no significance to the position of the arms and hands. But since we teach the kata piecemeal, a move at a time, students look for and assign meaning to "every inch" of kata.[6]

Separating the movement of the feet and hands facilitates learning for the beginner, but this initial rhythm becomes ingrained, repeated by even advanced students, leading to misunderstandings of the applications of the movements. Though it is taught a move at a time, in application the hand techniques that follow are meant to be done at the same time one steps forward into the above horse stance.

Your attacker has grabbed your wrist (1C). As you step to the northeast, on a 45-degree line from the attack and to the outside of the attacking arm, both hands are brought up simultaneously, back to back (1D & F). Your hand then rotates and grabs the opponent's wrist as his other hand, fist closed, is brought down on your attacker's elbow (1E &G). This arm-bar has the effect of bringing your opponent's head forward and down.

Traditionally, because the application of these kata moves has been left to the imagination and discovery of the student, this technique has generally been explained as a release against a two-handed chokehold or lapel grab. But it makes no practical sense to step forward towards an attacker who is applying a chokehold. However, to the beginning student, who is merely imitating movement when he learns kata, it looks as if both hands are doing the same thing. This is where our methodology—our general reticence in teaching principles—gets us into trouble.

The next hand technique in this sequence of moves has also been fundamentally misunderstood. The katas themselves, as in this hand technique, incorporate mnemonic devices to convey certain principles of movement; that is, certain kata movements are only intended to teach a beginning student how to move and were never meant to be used as applications.

In the hand movements that follow the previous closed-hand grab release and arm-bar (1A–G), both hands are brought up, wrists leading the way, the forward hand at shoulder level and the rear hand to the side of the chest (2A). Since most schools teach kata piecemeal, this palm-up position is seen as having no relationship to the previous technique; however, it is actually part of the same combination. Once the opponent's head has been brought forward and down with the arm-bar, the forward hand comes up to grab the attacker's head (2B & D). As the head is pulled in, the rear open hand is used to attack the opponent's neck or throat (2C & E). The initial palm-up position (2A) is used to remind the student that the elbow should be kept down.

There should be no pause between raising the hand and grabbing the opponent's head. The pause is only used in a teaching sense to check the student's technique, to check that the elbow has indeed been kept down as the hand comes up. This same palm-up movement can be found in a number of places in other Goju-Ryu katas, and the same explanation applies. It is not surprising that a Chinese-based system stresses this principle within its pedagogical forms. Classical Chinese martial texts also make a point of mentioning this. Yang Chengfu, the great taijiquan master, reminds us to keep "the elbows folded down," and Wu Yuxiang advises one to "sink the elbows," calling it one of the basic "body principles" (Wile, 1983: 6, 27).

When people fail to realize that the kata itself contains these teaching instructions—whether the teachers themselves have not learned them or students are left to their own devices in how they are to apply the techniques of kata—then each movement is thought to contain application techniques. This movement is often thought to be a chest block followed by a grab (2A & B). But the hand techniques are only separated to facilitate learning proper movement. They are not meant to imply separate applications. One can see, however, that this misconception is a natural outgrowth both of the method by which the movement is taught and the fact that the movement itself contains a mnemonic device that is meant to teach a principle of movement instead of an actual application.

Dissociation of Kata and Applications

While this next sequence of movements in Seiunchin kata (3A–F) may seem to have only a peripheral connection to the problems associated with teaching

methodology, the misunderstanding here results from the disconnection we bring to the training hall; we tend to disassociate kata movements from their applications.

In this sequence, after you have grabbed the head and attacked the throat of the opponent (2D–E), you shift to the left into a right-foot-forward cat stance, as the right hand twists and pulls the hair and the left hand grabs the chin (3A–B).[7] Then, shifting forward into a right-foot-forward basic stance, pushing the attacker forward and turning him around, with the right hand pulling the hair and the left hand twisting the chin (3C & E), the defender steps back into a left-foot-forward basic stance, bringing the right elbow up forcefully into the back of the head, neck, or spine (3D & F).

For whatever reason, these applications have not generally been passed on to students. We are dogmatic about preserving the movements of kata, but we tend to see the applications of kata as a creative endeavor, forgetting that the applications (*bunkai*) certainly came before the katas. Perhaps we don't wish to acknowledge the anachronistic nature of an empty hand combat system in modern times, at least the way that it is often studied today. In any case, this sequence of techniques has fed the imagination of students, particularly those raised on the belief that the study of applications is based more on invention than principle.

Failure to Separate Instructional Cues from Application

The next sequence of techniques—the second of the six combinations shown in Seiunchin kata—illustrates the failure to separate the instructional cues within the kata from the application techniques. Like the first sequence, this combination of moves is also a response against a wrist grab. The difference between the two is the strength or commitment of the attacker.

3D

3E

3F

The sequence begins with the right fist being brought into the palm of the left hand in front of the left hip (4A). The hands are then rotated in contact with each other until the right arm is brought across the body to a perpendicular position, elbow down and fist up at shoulder level, with the left palm held along the right wrist, fingers pointing up. At the same time, one steps into a right-foot-forward basic stance to the northeast (4B).

It has always been assumed that this technique demonstrates an assisted block against a very strong attacker who has stepped in with a right punch or has grabbed one's lapel with his right hand. That is, the right arm is blocking and the left palm is pushing against it for support. This is an example of a creative rationalization where there is no foundation of principles or understanding of the mistakes that can arise when one does not fully understand the instructions contained within the kata itself. The confusion comes, in this case, from a too literal interpretation of a movement, one that is ironically meant only to represent an application or to remind the student how the technique should be applied. The left open palm acts as a mnemonic device, reminding the student where on the opponent's body one is applying the technique. One can see the same methodology in Saifa and Sanseiru katas, where again the defender's hand in solo kata is positioned on the body to remind the student of where it will be applied on the attacker [see insets]. In any case, in this technique from Seiunchin kata, it should be clear that the left palm is not simply supporting the right arm, and the right arm is not blocking.

The attacker has grabbed your wrist (4C). Unlike the wrist grab in the first sequence of Seiunchin kata, your attacker here is very strong and locked down on your wrist. As the right hand is brought across to the left hip, the left hand grabs the attacker's wrist (4D). Then, holding onto his wrist, stepping into a right-foot-forward basic stance to the northeast, both hands are brought

across the body and up, freeing the right hand (4E). You now continue this sequence by stepping forward, into a left-foot-forward horse stance (*shiko dachi*), along the northeast line, driving your shoulder into your attacker and, breaking his balance, forcing him back and down (4F & H). Holding onto the opponent's wrist and dragging him back, you then step back along the same line, into a right-foot-forward horse stance, using the right forearm—in what is erroneously thought to be a down block—to attack the opponent's head or neck (4G & I).

Use of Mnemonic Teaching Devices

Another place where one can see the use of mnemonic teaching devices is the last sequence of Seiunchin kata. Here, you have just completed what are often referred to as two elbow techniques, though the primary function of each of these is a wrist or grab release. After the second of these, in right-foot-forward cat stance (*neko ashi dachi*) (5A–B), you reach over with the left hand to grab the opponent (5C–D). Then, shifting forward, you attack your opponent's collarbone with the right forearm (5E–F).

In the next move of this sequence, you step back into a left-foot-forward cat stance, bringing both open hands into a mountain block (*yama uke*) around the back of your opponent's head (5G–H). Again, because kata is so often taught piecemeal, without any understanding of its structuring principles, this technique has often been explained as a release against a two-handed lapel grab or choke hold. But this series of moves is fairly straightforward if it is executed as a combination of techniques against a single attacker; there should be no gaps in the execution of these techniques.

However, the final technique in this sequence is only implied in the kata. The cat stance acts as a kind of application mnemonic, indicating a knee kick (*hiza geri*). In general,

...yu classical katas, ...unter-attacking ...er than a kick, ...h the forearms ...ought around ...nd dropping ...nt's head is ...o bring the ...his then, ...ing tech-...nchin kata.

We tend to see mystery where there is only misunderstanding. In the absence of explanation, "secret" or "hidden techniques" (*kakushi-te*) have worked their way into the terminology of kata and the imaginations of students. It is tempting to embrace the mystery of kata as an insoluble conundrum even as we attempt to discover its secrets. After all, we are so often reminded that the journey is more important than the destination. But one should certainly be suspect of anything that purports to offer knowledge wrapped in the cloak of mystery. The Wizard of Oz hides behind a curtain woven of just such whole cloth. Better to unveil the problem, to examine the way we teach and to question what we don't know.

What I have found is that much of the confusion in the way we interpret kata techniques seems to be a natural by-product of the way we teach karate, the way it has always been taught. It has also led, I believe, to a misunderstanding of the patterns and directions of kata (Hopkins, 2004). And, because of the manner in which we dissect kata and train one-point sparring (*ippon kumite*), we have failed to see that katas are composed of combinations or sequences of techniques (Hopkins, 2002).

In certain cases, these differences of opinion or misunderstandings have occurred because some have indeed lost the formula necessary to understand the lessons of kata, but we also need to question our methods. Perhaps it is something rooted in Japanese culture not to question—something inherent in the ethos of martial training that stresses discipline and hard work, built on unquestioning loyalty and devotion to the teacher. On the other hand, there are few teachers, Japanese or American, willing to examine their own methodology, especially when that methodology is part of a long-standing tradition. To question any of this may sound somehow blasphemous. We seem to prefer mysticism to understanding, or at least it would seem so based on the way we teach and the way we study karate.

Notes

¹ Upon the death of Miyagi Chojun in 1953, Goju-Ryu split into a number of different schools, and over the course of the last half-century, even these schools have broken into different factions. Some researchers have suggested that an analysis of similar kata from different schools might provide valuable clues to the meaning of obscure moves in kata.

² This view that katas were used to hide information rather than convey techniques and teach the principles of a martial system seems to have some support in certain quarters. However, it doesn't seem at all logical that the old masters from long ago would hide information from students who had to be accepted by the master, under rigorous character scrutiny, in the first place.

³ All subsequent references to kata in this chapter refer not to modern training subjects like Gekisai Ichi but to the classical subjects and the teaching of these subjects—Saifa, Seiunchin, Shisochin, Sepai, Sanseiru, Sesan, Kururunfa, and Suparimpei—said to have originated in China, brought to Okinawa by Higaonna Kanryo.

⁴ Though it is outside the parameters of this chapter to go into a lengthy discussion of principles of bunkai, it may be useful to mention some in passing. For a more detailed explanation of some of these principles, see author's articles in earlier volumes of the *Journal of Asian Martial Arts*.

⁵ The kanji of Seiunchin is often translated as "control–pull–fight," but the English translation, as well as the kanji itself, has been the subject of some scholarly dispute, which, if nothing else, highlights the difficulties faced by any historical research into the origins of martial traditions. Translations range from "set of pushing and pulling" to "attack distant suppression" to "blue hawk battle." In light of the applications of this kata, however, some kanji and translations would appear to be more appropriate than others.

⁶ There are any number of texts available that will show this first position being used against a bear hug from the rear. There are, however, at least two problems with this interpretation. First, it is not the best or even a very effective technique to use against a bear hug from the rear. And second, the kata doesn't show what one does to the attacker after this; there is no counter-attack if one accepts this explanation of kata technique.

⁷ There is a strong historical component to some of the techniques preserved in the katas that has largely been ignored. As is evident here, these techniques were codified at a time in the past when men generally wore their hair longer or in topknots.

Bibliography

Babladelis, P. (1989). *Interview Meitoku Yagi (Goju Ryu)*. Retrieved on February 1, 2004, from http://www.xs4all.nl/~frits007/history/yagi.htm

Co, A. (1998). *Five ancestor fist kung-fu: The way of Ngo Cho Kun*. Rutland, Vermont: Charles E. Tuttle.

Craig, D. & Anderson, P. (2002). *Shihan-te: The bunkai of karate kata*. Boston, MA: YMAA Publication Center.

Heilman, C. (1997). *The dynamics of kata*. Retrieved on June 16, 2002, from http://www.ikkf.org/article4Q97.html

Higaonna, M. (February 2004). Suparimpei: Goju Ryu's supreme kata. *Classical Fighting Arts, (3)*, 5–10.

Hopkins, G. (2002). The lost secrets of Goju-Ryu: What the kata shows. *Journal of Asian Martial Arts, 11(4)*, 54–77.

Hopkins, G. (2004). The shape of kata: The "enigma" of pattern. *Journal of Asian Martial Arts, 13(1)*, 64–77.

Labbate, M. (2000). Developing advanced Goju-Ryu techniques. *Journal of Asian Martial Arts, 9(1)*, 56–69.

McCarthy, P. (Trans.) (1995). *The bible of karate: Bubishi*. Rutland, VT: Charles E. Tuttle.

McCarthy, P. *Kata: The enigma of Uchinadi*. Posted on August 26, 2001, at http://www.fightingarts.com/forums/ubb/Forum10/HTML/000008.html

McCarthy, P. The theory and practice of tradition [sic] karate. Retrieved on January 23, 2002, from http://www.society.webcentral.com.au/Secrets.htm

Schoene, M. (15 Jan. 2004). *Interview with Anthony Mirakian Sensei*. Retrieved on January 15, 2004, from http://home.achilles.net/~pchan/ amintvw.html

Toguchi, S. (2001). *Okinawan Goju-Ryu: Advanced techniques of Shorei-kan karate*. Santa Clarita, CA: Ohara Publications.

Wile, D. (1983). *T'ai-chi touchstones: Yang family secret transmissions*. New York: Sweet Ch'i Press.

Acknowledgment

A special thanks to John Jackson, Ole Craig, and Brian Conz for their help in demonstrating applications for this article, and to my teacher, Kimo Wall. Also, a special thanks to my wife, Martha, for her editorial assistance and patience. Giles Hopkins can be reached at Kodokan3@Juno.com.

The Five Katas
of Yagi Meitoku

by Perry Campbell, B.Sc.

A photograph of Yagi Meitoku in 1985,
the year of his 75th birthday. Master Yagi
gave this print to Paul Babladelis in 1989.

All other photographs courtesy of P. Campbell.

Introduction

The passing of Grand Master (*Dai Sensei*) Yagi Meitoku at 91 (February 7, 2003) signified the end of an era in the art of Goju-Ryu, leaving a great hole in the Okinawan martial arts community. Mr. Yagi traced his ancestry back to the original thirty-six Chinese families who moved to the Kume district of Naha, Okinawa, more than six hundred years ago, bringing with them, among many things, their martial arts. Yagi Meitoku's love, dedication, and passion for Goju-Ryu karate and his teacher, Miyagi Chojun, radiated from him. Mr. Yagi dedicated his life to teaching Goju-Ryu's advanced techniques well into his 80's. He left five katas, the Meibuken katas, as his contribution to Goju-Ryu karate: Heaven and Earth (*Tenshi*) and the four mythical guardians that protect them: Blue Dragon (*Seiryu*), White Tiger (*Byakko*), Red Sparrow (*Shujakku*), and Black Turtle (*Genbu*). Deceptively simple in format, yet layered with complex theories, the Meibuken katas are Yagi Meitoku's record of the fighting practices, techniques, drills, and innovations he developed over a lifetime of study.

Miyagi's Successor

Upon Miyagi Chojun's passing (October 8, 1953), there were a small group of individuals who felt they were the rightful heirs to the Goju-Ryu system: Higa Seko, Miyazato Ei'ichi, Miyagi An'ichi, and Miyagi Chojun's son, Kei. Despite the fact that Miyagi never chose a successor or issued rank to any of his students before his death, very few seniors of the other major Okinawan karate systems disputed Yagi Meitoku's claim as the heir. In the end, the responsibility of choosing a successor fell on the shoulders of Miyagi Chojun's wife and children. According to Miyagi Masu (Tsuru), Miyagi's eldest daughter, choosing Yagi was not difficult. In a letter translated in Ernest Estrada's *Interviews*, Tsuru said:

> I respect him [Yagi] very much and so does the Miyagi family. Upon my father's death, the family met to discuss who would succeed my father as head of Goju-Ryu. The decision was based on who studied the longest, and who was the most dedicated and loyal to my father. It was then that Meitoku Yagi was decided upon to head Goju-Ryu. At that time we decided to formally recognize him by giving him my father's karate uniform and belt.

Mr. Yagi's son, Meitetsu, confirmed his father's loyalty to Miyagi. Meitetsu said he could remember each time a typhoon struck Okinawa while Miyagi was alive:

> My father would first go to Miyagi's home to close the shutters and prepare for the storm. Only after Miyagi's home was secure would father return to prepare our home.

To certify the Miyagi family's choice of Yagi Meitoku as the second grandmaster of the Goju-Ryu system, they presented him with Miyagi's uniform (*dogi*). Tsuru said:

> It was felt that instructor Yagi was the best person to carry on my father's teachings. So he was asked to continue my father's teachings and also to expand on the teachings so that everyone would know Goju-Ryu.

33

Training with Miyagi Chojun

Yagi Meitoku was 12 years old when his grandfather took him to Miyagi Chojun's school to begin formal training. At that time, there were five or six students senior to Yagi, including Higa Seko, Nakaima Genkai, Azama Kasai (Nanjo Kiju), Toguchi Seikichi, and Sakiyama Tatsutoku.

Instructor Yagi said they did many repetitions of preparatory exercises (*yobi undo*) with each student, counting 100 to 1,000 repetitions of each technique. It was very demanding and most new students went elsewhere to look for easier training. In those early days, Miyagi taught only four katas: Sanchin, Sesan, Seiunchin, and Tensho. These were the open hand (*kaishu*) katas. Of these forms, Seiunchin and Sesan were considered the training katas and had to be studied thoroughly to understand Goju-Ryu. Yagi was among the first of Miyagi's students to learn all the katas, including Saifa, Shisochin, Sanseiryu, Sepai, Kururunfa, and Suparimpei, which Miyagi started teaching when Yagi was in his first year of junior high school.

Instructor Yagi said it would take four to five years before they even began learning the kata. Then Miyagi would teach them only one kata for two or more years. He said Sanchin training was particularly severe. Yagi recounted how people would recognize him as a student of Miyagi just from the bruises on his shoulders from Miyagi's severe testing in Sanchin.

In His Later Years

I first met Master Yagi in 1988. I recall wondering what would he be like. Would he be fierce or impatient? I had heard stories of his awesome power. He often broke punching boards (*makiwara*) at will. How he had seemingly little to do with other Goju-Ryu styles. So it was a shock that he was nothing like I'd expected him to be. Mr. Yagi was soft spoken, friendly, and tranquil, very much like my grandfather had been. Yet, his eyes were sharp and could change at will into something to be feared, exemplifying his killing stare (*koroshi no mei*). The muscles under the aging skin were amazingly powerful and he moved with graceful fluidity and speed despite his advanced years.

In 1990, when I moved to Okinawa, it was immediately apparent that Yagi's passion had not ebbed. By then he had retired from formal teaching, yet he continued to teach three children's classes each week—a group that he had surprisingly little control over. He would also instruct foreigners in the mornings. The foreigners' visits would generally last two or three weeks. Since I was living there, however, he worked with me each morning and then again in the afternoon, six and seven days a week. Further, he would allow my participation in the children's classes. During this period, despite his occasional bouts with poor health, he would not only come to the dojo to teach two and three times a day, he would practice daily. It was during this period that I began to see how remarkable Yagi Meitoku really was.

At 80, Yagi was deceptively fluid and quick, and he still possessed great power. Yet there was more to him. He regularly played piano and violin. He was a master calligrapher. In 1988, he was the Japanese champion of Chinese chess (*Chunji*). In 1989, he defended his title and became world champion as well. Not surprisingly, his mastery of strategy carried into his martial arts theories, technique, and applications. They are also were embedded within his five Meibuken katas.

Influences

Some have said that Mr. Yagi taught the kata "exactly" as Miyagi Chojun taught him, however, this was not the case. As the Miyagi family requested, Yagi Meitoku spent his entire life studying and expanding upon his teacher's teachings. There are several nuances and finer points of the Goju-Ryu kata he developed in his later years. Some of these alterations came after even some of his senior students had opened their own schools. Hence, not all of his direct students practice some of his innovations.

In addition to his teacher, Miyagi Chojun, Yagi credited two men who influenced his innovations, although there may have been others. The first was his friend, Ko Shinko—a Chinese martial arts master from Taiwan who is also recognized as having introduced conditioning drills (*kotikitai*) to Okinawan karate. The second was another close friend, Taira Shinken, the weapons master and president of the Ryukyu Kobudo Hozoin Shinkokai. Although each innovation Yagi incorporated was subtle, each notably increased the technique's strength and effectiveness. Not only do the Meibuken katas expand upon Goju-Ryu's techniques, they also include the influences of these two men.

The Chinese influence in the Meibuken katas is immediately apparent from the first movement. Yagi Meitoku incorporated the Chinese style of bow and opening—feet are shoulder width apart, hands form a triangle in front of the body at chin level, with the right hand a fist and the left open (a representation of the Chinese character for the Ming Dynasty). The most significant import from the Chinese system, however, is the idea of putting two solo forms together to create a two-man set with almost no alterations to the original forms. At a basic level, these sets contain striking, kicking, and grappling techniques, all executed in continuous motion from beginning to end. At deeper levels, the applications are brutally efficient.

The author with
Yagi Meitoku in
Okinawa, 1988.

Deceptive Brilliance

I think the two most remarkable aspects of Mr. Yagi's katas is the secret way they pair—*Seiryu/Byakko, Shujakku/Genbu,* and *Tenshi*)—fitting together to be practiced as two-man sets. The second is that he developed these kata in his head (bearing in mind that the second kata of each set must be performed reversed—in the mirror image—to make them work together). He did this without the benefit of a partner to ensure that they would be synchronized. These are clear indicators of Yagi's advanced understanding of strategy.

The Five Meibuken Katas

Heaven and Earth

Originally called *Fukyo Kata I and II,* Heaven and Earth (*Tenshi*) was Yagi's first Meibuken kata. In the book *Okinawan Karate-do Goju-Ryu Meibukan* by Yagi Meitetsu, Carl Wheeler, and Brock Vickerson (1998), Yagi said, "I first got the idea for this kata following a visit to Taiwan." Tenshi is one kata when split into two halves—Heaven and Earth—the halves fit together to form a short two-man set. The kata is characterized by open-hand and finger strikes, double strikes, wrist throws, and scooping the leg. Developed in 1974, Tenshi was an experiment that proved a success and paved the way for the next four Meibuken katas.

Blue Dragon

Blue Dragon (*Seiryu*) is the mythical guardian of the west. The form is characterized by knee kicks, percussion strikes, and powerful waist and hip rotations used in the generation of power in both blocking and striking. Blue Dragon couples with White Dragon to form a two-man set. Thus it contains the attacks and counterattacks for White Dragon.

The rotation of the hips and waist in the wrist block/punch/low block combination is conducted around the body's center axis, with the body upright. Mr. Yagi frequently used a short trident (*sai*) as a model to demonstrate the rotation. Holding the *sai* perpendicular to the ground, handle upwards, he would rotate the *sai* clockwise and counterclockwise in his hand. The rotating tangs clearly demonstrate the rotation he wanted.

White Tiger

White Tiger (*Byakko*) is the mythical guardian of the east. The form's techniques are the opposite of those in Blue Dragon. White Tiger is characterized by powerful punching techniques, utilizing upward and downward movement to generate power. This is accomplished by dropping rapidly from a high stance to a low stance, and then springing back to a high stance. The power generated through this dropping and springing proves effective against those of Blue Dragon, which as mentioned utilizes rotation. White Tiger also introduces defending against an attack to the knee.

Red Sparrow

Red Sparrow (*Shujakku*) is Okinawa's mythical guardian of the north. The kata is characterized by open-hand strikes, feinting, rapid hand/foot combinations, and escaping grabbing and locking attacks. When worked as part of the two-man set with its partner, Black Turtle, Red Sparrow is light and quick—like the bird it is named after—and elusive to Black Turtle's grappling holds.

Interestingly, the origin of Red Sparrow's final movement is the same as the second to last movement of Miyagi's original version of Tensho—Heishu Kata Tensho—which Yagi resurrected in early 1991.

Black Turtle

Black Turtle (*Genbu*) is the mythical guardian of the south. This form was completed in late 1990 and is Mr. Yagi's last kata. The mate for Red Sparrow, Black Turtle is characterized by the use of dropping into low, solid stances for blocking and striking. But at times, one springs up to a standing position to deliver a devastating blow. The kata also incorporates grappling. When practiced with Red Sparrow, the grappling and counters flow freely between strikes. This kata's techniques are strong and powerful.

Black Turtle's last movement is also the final movement of Miyagi's Tensho —Heishu Gata Tensho. According to Yagi, the final two movements are actually a Chinese exercise for increasing longevity. Their martial applications, however, are a full Nelson and its counter-technique.

Black Turtle & Red Sparrow

(Genbu and Shujakku)

The first movements of these two katas with their corresponding partner sequences.

Left: Both the Black Turtle and Red Sparrow katas commence with a formal bow.
Right: Partners pair off in the combined Black Turtle and Red Sparrow katas.

Photograph Column Layout

Left side: Black Turtle. Right side: Red Sparrow. Paired: Black Turtle / Red Sparrow

Black Turtle — Black Turtle / Red Sparrow — Red Sparrow

40

Blue Dragon & White Tiger

(Seiryu and Byakko)

The first six movements of these two katas with their corresponding partner sequences, beginning with a formal bow.

Blue Dragon / White Tiger

Blue Dragon

White Tiger

White Tiger   Blue Dragon / White Tiger   Blue Dragon

Advanced Applicatons from Heaven and Earth Kata

(Tenshi)

Tenshi's first movement and application.

Two later movements found in Tenshi kata and possible applications.

Advanced Applicaton from Red Sparrow Kata

The photograph on the left shows the solo movement in the kata, followed by the series which shows a takedown.

Below, (1) the entry movement,
       (2) set-up and
       (3) finishing take-down.

The Legacy

Yagi Meitoku and his peers are from a period that has been called "the Golden Age of karate." With their passing, the last remnants of their era are disappearing as well. Yet all has not been lost. Along with Yagi Meitoku's direct students who continue his teachings, Yagi Sensei has left a tangible record of some of his knowledge, techniques, theories, and innovations in his Meibuken katas.

A Preliminary Analysis of
Goju-Ryu Kata Structure

by Fernando Portela Câmara, Ph.D. & Mario McKenna, M.Sc.

Higaonna Kanryo and his student Kyoda Juhatsu (left).
All photographs courtesy of Mario McKenna.

Introduction

Goju-Ryu is the name of a karatedo style Miyagi Chojun (1888–1953) organized in the 1930's. Miyagi alleged that his system originated from a Chinese *quanfa* (*gongfu*) school established in the city of Naha in 1828 (Miyagi, 1934) and credited Higaonna Kanryo (1853–1917) as the primary source of the system. Yet when we examine modern Goju-Ryu we can see several important influences on its development. These include the modern karate method developed by Itosu Ankoh (1830–1916), the indigenous "Okinawa hand" (*ti* or *te*) tradition and Miyagi's personal studies.[1] We will discuss each of these briefly below.

Itosu taught the first karate classes publicly as part of elementary school physical education curriculum in 1901 and later on at the junior high school level (Iwai, 1992; Okinawa Prefectural Board of Education, 1994).[2] Itosu's method included a number of key points (Kinjo, 1999; Murakami, 1991):

1) the development of a new series of introductory katas named Pinan,

2) the standardization of existing katas,

3) the emphasis on mental and physical discipline,

4) the cultivation of morality, and

5) the de-emphasis on pure combative technique (Kinjo, 1999; Murakami, 1991).

Itosu's method was continued and improved upon by subsequent students and teachers such as Funakoshi Gichin, Chibana Chosin, and Mabuni Kenwa; and formed the basis for modern Okinawa and Japanese karate.

The influence of Itosu's method on Miyagi was critical to the future development of Goju-Ryu. According to Kinjo Hiroshi, Goju-Ryu is a modern style in line with Itosu's karate model (Kinjo, 2007). Kinjo argues that both Itosu and Higaonna organized karate in 1905, however only Itosu's model was adopted by the Okinawa Prefecture Education Department. It was rumored that because of Higaonna's focus on Sanchin kata training that it was considered unsuitable for developing adolescents (Kinjo, 2007). That coupled with another rumor that Higaonna drank excessively stopped Higaonna's karate from being introduced into the school system. Miyagi was a student at the first prefecture junior high school during the time that the Itosu model of karate was introduced and would have learned karate from Itosu and his student Hanashiro Chomo.

Itosu Anko—The person most responsible for modernizing karatedo.

As an adult, Miyagi organized the karate that he had learned from Higaonna and had it accepted as part of the Okinawa prefecture commercial school. This was Miyagi's karate which he would later call Goju-Ryu. It is interesting to speculate if one of Miyagi's motivations for having Goju-Ryu introduced into the school system was the memory of his teacher's grief and the early popularity of Itosu's karate.

In contrast to karatedo, *ti* is a pre-World War II generic term referring to the non-kata based unarmed combative traditions practiced on Okinawa (Hokama, 1999). It does not refer to a specific method, system, or style of combat. The oral tradition of the older Okinawan karate teachers refers to postures, stances, techniques, etc. with the generic term *ti*. Interestingly, according to Higaonna Morio, Miyagi Chojun only referred to what he taught as *ti* (Higaonna, 1998).

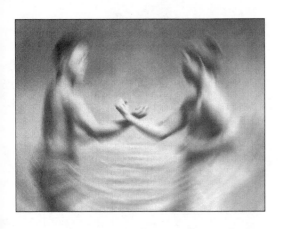

A young Miyagi Chojun (left)
and Kyoda Juhatsu
demonstrating techniques.

Lastly, there are several, but under-documented accounts of Miyagi Chojun researching other fighting systems. When investigating Miyagi Chojun's life, we see that he spent most of his life's energies and his family fortune to studying the fighting arts. During his studies he came into contact with such fighting traditions as Fujian White Crane boxing (*baihequan*), Tiger boxing (*huquan*), Monk Fist boxing (*Lohanquan*), and possibly Five Ancestor fist boxing (*wuzuquan*) (Kinjo, 1999; Tokashiki, 1991). This raises questions regarding the continuity in the kata passed on by Miyagi Chojun.

Goju-Ryu's Kata Catalog

In the late 1930's, Goju-Ryu apparently consisted of eight katas: Seiunchin, Saifa, Shisochin, Sanseru, Sepai, Sesan, Kururunfa, and Suparimpei/Pechurin; and two basic exercises that were adapted into a kata format, Sanchin and Tensho. In the early 1940's, two basic introductory katas were added to the system: Gekisai I and II.

Kanzaki Shigekazu (b. 1928) and Murakami Katsumi (b. 1927) were disciples of Kyoda Juhatsu (1887–1968), a long-time student of Higaonna and Miyagi's senior. Both men claim that Higaonna Kanryo taught only the Sanchin, Sesan, Sanseru, and Pechurin katas. Examining these four forms reveals that each kata has an asymmetric pattern. That is, kicks are done predominantly with the right leg and upper body techniques are frequently done with only one side of the body.

The Seiunchin, Saifa, Shisochin, Sepai, and Kururunfa katas are of note in comparison to the four previously mentioned katas, as they are symmetric forms. Kicks and techniques are frequently done with both sides of the body. Seiunchin, Sepai, and Kururunfa are mentioned in the late 1930's in the written works of Mabuni Kenwa (1889–1951), a karate teacher and friend of Miyagi. Miyagi's early students also mention Seiunchin as one of the older katas he taught. In contrast, Shisochin and Saifa are not mentioned in any published karate list of the 1920's or 1930's. Interestingly, Miyagi was apparently the only person to pass on these five katas.

46

Alternate Sources

There appears to be a lack of written documentation on the origin and transmission of Goju-Ryu katas. In addition, testimonies from older teachers are filled with contradictions and inconsistencies. Taking this into account, the origins and lineage of Goju-Ryu kata remain unclear.

According to noted martial arts historian Hokama Tetsuhiro (Hokama, 1999), there are six ways to analyze Okinawan karatedo katas:

1) methods of walking, hand use, and technique utilization,
   e.g. Sanchin, Shisochin;
2) names of the founder or originator of a particular tradition
   e.g. Kusanku, Wansu, etc.;
3) names of specific areas or districts in which the tradition was
   practiced, e.g. Shuri, Naha, Tomari;
4) the religious or spiritual principles inherent within a tradition,
   e.g. Suparimpei, Sepai;
5) the metaphysical or transcendental aspects of a tradition
   (catharsis / purification / Zen), e.g. Sanchin, Tensho; and
6) the implied movement of animals.

Of these six methods, the analysis of methods of walking, hand use, and technique utilization in Goju-Ryu katas may provide an interesting and useful means of investigating their origin and development. In this paper, the structure of the eight Goju-Ryu katas will be analyzed by the exploratory statistical technique of cluster analysis to obtain a classification of these katas and formulate ideas about their origins.

Data Mining

Data mining can be defined as the science of extracting useful information from large data sets. In other words, data mining provides a practical means for the classification and distinction of large amounts of data. We can think of data mining by using an analogy of mining for gold. A data miner looks for "gold" (useful knowledge and information) by "striking ore" (mountains of data) by using different kinds of tools (such as a statistical technique). Data mining then is a technique to help us distinguish gold from ore.

In order for us to "mine the data" contained in the Goju-Ryu katas, we classified each kata on the basis of repeated patterns or themes found in them. Goju-Ryu katas show a recurrence of patterns that can be used as an inventory for classification. For example, the following characteristics can be observed in the original Higaonna katas (Sesan, Sanseru, and Pechurin/Suparimpei) as stated by Kanzaki and Murakami:

1) all begin with three steps forward from the Sanchin exercise,
2) all have a four directional (or cross) performance pattern,
3) two of them (Sesan and Pechurin/Suparimpei) have three steps in Sanchin stance while performing double open-hand blocks (*osae-uke* and *sukui-uke*).

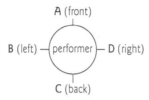

In addition, these katas have associated asymmetries:

1) kicks are performed with the right leg;
2) punches are concluded with the left fist.

In contrast, Saifa, Shisochin, Sepai, Kururunfa, and Seiunchin are symmetrical katas. Shisochin, Saifa, and Seiunchin begin with three advancing steps while repeating the same technique, but do not follow the Sanchin stance or pattern. The majority of techniques from these five katas are performed with both sides of the body, making them symmetrical.

Based on these observations, two senior Goju-Ryu instructors identified ten themes among Goju-Ryu katas. Each kata was then rated by the instructors for the presence (1) or absence (0) of each theme (Table 1). The predominant theme was symmetry of a kata and was defined as the percentage of repeated techniques with both sides of the body. A kata was considered symmetrical if it had greater than 20% repetition of techniques on both sides of the body.

Left: Opening movement from the Seiunchin kata.

Right: Knee kick (*kansetsugeri*).

48

Only the classical katas were used, as these are the forms that have been thought to have been passed down from Higaonna Kanryo to Miyagi Chojun. Therefore, the Sanchin, Tensho, and Gekisai katas were not included in this analysis. Tensho and Gekisai were excluded as they are modern exercises while Sanchin has almost complete symmetry.

TABLE 1: Occurrence of Patterns in the Classical Goju-Ryu Katas

NOTE: Sanchin = Sanchin Pattern; Sesan = Sesan pattern; Three-theme = beginning kata with three repetitions; Cross pattern = Four directional pattern; Maegeri = front kick; Kansetsugeri = low side kick; Nidangeri = double kick; Other kicks = other kicks; Assym. kicks = kicks done with only with right leg; Symmetry = >20% of repetition for both sides.

Themes / Kata	Sanseru	Sesan	Suparimpei	Saifa
1. Sanchin	I	I	I	0
2. Sesan	0	I	I	0
3. Three-theme	I	I	I	I
4. Cross pattern	I	I	I	0
5. Maegeri	I	I	I	I
6. Kansetsugeri	I	I	0	0
7. Nidangeri	I	0	I	0
8. Other kicks	I	I	I	0
9. Assym. kicks	I	I	I	0
10. Symmetry	0	0	0	I

Themes / Kata	Seiunchin	Shisochin	Sepai	Kururunfa
1. Sanchin	0	I	0	0
2. Sesan	0	0	0	I
3. Three-theme	I	I	0	0
4. Cross pattern	0	I	0	0
5. Maegeri	0	I	I	I
6. Kansetsugeri	0	0	0	0
7. Nidangeri	0	0	0	0
8. Other kicks	0	0	0	0
9. Assym. kicks	0	0	0	0
10. Symmetry	I	I	I	I

Left: Scooping block (*sukui uke*).
Right: Sanchin stance—a fundamental
posture found in Goju-Ryu and
katas from the Naha city area.

A cluster analysis was then performed. Cluster analysis allows for the classification of different things or objects into similar groups (clusters). The analysis separates each kata into a different group so that one kata is more similar with others within its group compared with other katas outside its group. This allows the separation of data into meaningful sets that share common characteristics. Cluster analysis forms a tree-like structure known as a dendogram to visually show the groupings of different things, in this instance kata. The clusters analysis was performed using the statistical program SPSS (V14.0).[3] These techniques allowed for the classification of Goju-Ryu katas to provide insight about their structure.

Results and Discussion

Cluster analysis based on the categorization of themes in Table 1 revealed that the classical katas consisted of two clusters (Figures 1). The first cluster included Sanseru, Sesan, and Superimpei/Pechurin. The second cluster included Saifa, Seiunchin, Shisochin, Sepai, and Kururunfa. The first cluster was labeled the Higaonna cluster (Cluster H). The second cluster was labeled the Miyagi cluster (Cluster M). This raises some important questions in the development of modern Goju-Ryu as formulated by Miyagi Chojun.

Right: Front kick (*maegeri*).

FIGURE 1 Tree Diagram for the Eight Classical Goju-Ryu Katas

Complete Linkage, Squared Euclidean Distances

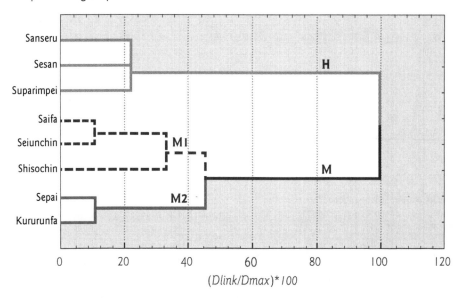

The above chart visually portrays the results of the cluster analysis. It is referred to as a dendrogram or a tree-like diagram. This shows the relationship between the different katas and the groups they form. We can see that the Higaonna or Cluster H (50% black line) consists of Sanseru, Sesan and Suparimpei/Pechurin. In contrast we can see the Miyagi or Cluster M (black line) consists of Saifa, Seiunchin, Shisochin, Sepai and Kururunfa. Looking closer we can see that the analysis broke down the Cluster M further into two smaller groups: Cluster M1 (dash line) which contains Saifa, Seiunchin and Shisochin, and Cluster M2 (70% black line) which contains Sepai and Kururunfa.

First, could Cluster H be considered an indigenous boxing method while Cluster M be considered Chinese boxing? On March 19, 1866, the last group of Chinese envoys visited Okinawa. Documented within the program of this last visit was a demonstration of boxing and weaponry by Aragaki Seisho[4] and others at the Ochayagoten[5] in Shuri Castle. Several kata names were listed including Sesan and Suparimpei/ Pechurin (McKenna, 2001). Both of these katas are part of Cluster H. Therefore, these two katas were practiced on Okinawa before Higaonna Kanryo reportedly left for China and could be considered indigenous. We can hypothesize that due to the grouping of katas in Cluster H, that Sanchin and Sanseru may also have been practiced during this time, suggesting that Cluster H represents an Okinawan boxing method. Further corroborating evidence can be seen if we examine the curriculum of Kyoda Juhatsu's To'onryu which contains only four kata: Sanchin, Sesan, Sanseru and Pechurin. Therefore, we can speculate that Cluster H may represent the original Nahate kata (Sanchin, Sesan, Sanseru, and Suparimpei/Pechurin) as argued by Kanzaki and Murakami.

51

Second, these results suggest that Higaonna Kanryo was responsible for the introduction of Cluster H, but there is no clear proof that he was responsible for the introduction of Cluster M. The other katas found in Cluster M seem to be from different system(s) from the original four as found in Cluster H, and seem to be more of an addition to that curriculum rather than an integral part. We can also state that Cluster M appears for the first time as part of Miyagi Chojun's teachings.

It could be argued that the four original kata of Cluster H were beginner forms and only Miyagi Chojun learned the other more advanced forms found in Cluster M. However, as Hirakami (2001) points out, looking at the technical content of the four katas found in Cluster H, it is difficult to maintain this theory. Therefore, it is interesting to theorize that Cluster M represents newer Chinese katas introduced by Miyagi Chojun after Higaonna's death in 1915.

Finally, if Higaonna Kanryo taught the katas that form Cluster M only to Miyagi Chojun, then Higaonna passed on two or more different systems. That is, Higaonna passed on a modified version of what constitutes the original fighting arts of the Naha City area as represented by the Sanchin, Sesan, Sanseru, and Suparimpei/Pechurin katas. This then begs the question, where did these additional katas come from? Did they originate from Higaonna's teacher in China, Ryu Ryu Ko, or did they perhaps come from someone else?

Notes

[1] The characters used by Itosu to render karate would be pronounced *toudi* in Okinawan dialect, meaning "Tang/China Hand" showing a Chinese origin or influence.

[2] Although this is contradicted in Higaonna Morio's book, *The History of Karate: Okinawan Goju-Ryu* (1998).

[3] In SPSS (V14.0), the cluster analysis uses the average linkage as an algorithm for amalgamation and squared Euclidian distances.

[4] Aragaki Seisho (1840–1920) is considered to be Higaonna Kanryo's first boxing teacher.

[5] The royal tea house located in Shuri Castle.

Bibliography – English

Higaonna, M. (1998). *The history of karate: Okinawan Goju-Ryu*. Thousand Oaks, CA: Dragon Books.

McKenna, M. (2001). Exploring Goju Ryu's past: Myths and facts surrounding

Higashionna Kanryo, pt. 1–2. *Dragon Times*, 18–19.

McCarthy, P. (1993). *An outline of karatedo*. International Ryukyu Karate Research Society.

Bibliography – Japanese

Hirakami, N. (2001, May). Secret of Nafadi and Fujian boxing, pt. 1–2. *Gekkan Hiden*, 110–114.

Hokama, T. (1999). *Okinawa karate-do kobudo no shinzui*. Naha: Naha Shuppansha.

Iwai, T. (1992). *The ancient transmission of karate-jutsu*. Tokyo: Aiyudo.

Kinjo, A. (1999). *A true record of the transmission of karate*. Okinawa: Tosho Center.

Kinjo, H. (2007). Seitokukai homepage. http://skrt.s43.xrea.com/karatejp/modules/xoopsfaq/index.php?cat_id=7

Murakami, K. (1991). *The heart and technique of karate*. Tokyo: Shinjin Butsu Orai Sha Hakko.

Okinawa Prefectural Board of Education. (1994). *A basic investigative report into karatedo and kobudo*. Ginowan: Yojusha.

Tokashiki, I. (1991). *Gohaku-kai yearbook* (Vol. 4). Naha: n.p.

Acknowledgements

Thanks to Fred Lohse III for proofing and editing the manuscript; and Justin Chin, Maik Hassel, and Oliver Riche for posing for the photographs.

Kata & Bunkai:
A Study in Theme & Variations
in Karate's Solo Practice Routines

by Giles Hopkins, M.A.

Training implements in the dojo.
All photos courtesy of G. Hopkins.

Introduction

Late arrivals had simply kicked off their shoes, thinking no one would notice such a small breech of etiquette. Shoes were piled on top of shoes—mostly sandals and sneakers broken down at the heel. As the children's class came to an end, more and more children jostled their way through the entrance, deftly slipping on shoes and running off into the evening. Adult students were arriving, more serious than their young counterparts, their shoes forming neat rows, each pair facing out towards the street.

Inside, adults were silently stretching and warming up. One was doing exercises with the stone weights (*chishi*), while another was walking up and down the floor with the gripping jars (*nigirigame*). I was familiar with the gripping jars: how the hands spread across the openings of the jars, the sides of the thumbs just catching the lip of the opening. But it was on that first trip to Okinawa in 1986 where I realized that training with the jars, more than just an exercise in posture and stance work or even hand and finger strength, was a silent reminder of how important the grasping hand is to Okinawan karate. Like the tiger—one of the animals that the Goju-Ryu katas are said to be based on—once the prey is within his grasp, the Goju-Ryu practitioner doesn't let go until the opponent is down and no longer a threat. The techniques of the katas, I began to realize, were meant to show these grabs and controlling hands. But as is so often the case, we see the movements and the hand positions in katas without knowing what we're seeing. Like everyone else, we had studied katas, but we hadn't really seen them.

Photograph of
Giles Hopkins with Takamine Choboku
and Higa Seikichi at Higa's home in 1986.

That first summer in Okinawa we saw a lot we didn't fully understand; in fact, it raised more questions than it answered. The Okinawans seemed to move differently; everything was less rigid. Stances were generally higher. There were even noticeable differences in the classical katas. Why did one dojo start Kururunfa kata on the right and another dojo start it on the left? What we had practiced as a back-knuckle strike (*uraken*) in Sepai now looked more like a downward elbow or forearm strike. Where we did a front kick (*maegeri*) in Sanseiru, the Okinawans merely used a knee kick (*hizageri*). There seemed to be endless examples of these differences, and not just differences between what we had practiced in America and what was being done in Okinawa. There were also considerable differences between the various Okinawan schools.

55

When I asked Gibo Seki why the Higa dojo (Shodokan) started Kururunfa to the right and the Miyazato dojo (Jundokan) started it to the left, he merely replied, "Why not?" It was as if to say these were insignificant differences, leaving me with the feeling that I had asked not a stupid question but the wrong question. On yet another occasion, I asked him why there were so many apparent differences between the Shodokan (the school of Goju-Ryu founded by Higa Seko) version of Sanseiru and the Shoreikan (the school of Goju-Ryu founded by Toguchi Seikichi) version. Both teachers, after all, had studied with Miyagi Chojun (as, of course, had Miyazato Ei'ichi). How could the same kata look so different? But again Gibo seemed to brush off my question with a laugh. "I know seven different versions of Sanseiru," he said.[1]

There are numerous examples to illustrate this rather perplexing conundrum—that the same classical Goju-Ryu katas are done differently by different schools and dojos even within Okinawa. While some of these differences are certainly important and may lead one to vastly different interpretations of kata applications (bunkai), many are rather inconsequential. It is, in fact, easy to get distracted by differences that are really insignificant. Even old-school karate practitioners engage in seemingly endless discussions generated by superficial observations of differences in individual katas—this school starts to the left and that one starts to the right; they use basic stance (sanchin dachi) while this other school uses front stance (zenkutsu dachi); this school goes straight back and that one goes at an angle.

More often than not, one of my teacher's teachers, Matayoshi Shinpo (a master of Kingai-Ryu, Shorin-Ryu, Goju-Ryu, and kobudo), would meet these differences with a simple, "Yeah, okay." Most of these differences didn't seem to surprise him. But the journey to Okinawa for any student of karate must be at least in part a confirmation, a journey to make sure one is on the right path. If we are not meant to get answers to all of our questions, we may at least hope that there are enough signs to tell us that we're headed in the right direction. Of course it's in the nature of the martial arts itself that nothing is given away without hard work; there are no short cuts, and no easy answers. Perhaps the only surprise nowadays is that there

aren't as many shoes piled up outside the entrance to the dojo—after all, this is the birthplace of karate. But the kids are off playing baseball on dirt playgrounds behind the schools, and the adults are often too busy.

Giles Hopkins and his wife Martha at Matayoshi's house in 1988.

Questioning Kata

In Okinawa that summer, I may have been the only one disturbed by these differences. It seemed to me at the time that the classical Goju-Ryu katas should be done the same no matter what branch of Goju-Ryu one practiced, since all of the founding teachers had studied with Miyagi Chojun or at least with someone who had learned from him. Furthermore, if applications (*bunkai*) are clearly predicated on a kata's movements, one would think that any alteration of the kata's movements would affect one's understanding of application. Katas, after all, should dictate the applications, not the other way round. In some schools, the katas' movements seem to have been informed by someone's personal and perhaps idiosyncratic ideas for application. It is the nature of applications (*bunkai*), however, to be taken from a strict interpretation of the kata's movements. So it is probably still important to find "authentic" katas—what underscores the importance of lineage but whose lineage?

Additionally, I suspect, logic should provide another sort of barometer since one would expect how one interprets the movements of kata to reinforce the principles found throughout the system; many techniques, after all, show similarity though not necessarily sameness. This, of course, begs the question: If a technique seems to have no other references in other katas is it therefore suspect? Or is it simply unique? Or has it been changed out of either ignorance or a teacher's individual interpretation? But such a debate about which school is right and which is wrong, which kata is more authentic or which has been changed, is really unresolvable at this point.

It is far more instructive to compare similarities between the different katas of a system like Goju-Ryu than to compare the differences between different schools. This is a key point. Let me reiterate this. It is often more useful to examine the similarities between movements in different katas than it is to emphasize the differences of how one school and another school perform the same kata. By this I don't mean superficial differences such as which katas end in cat stance (*neko ashi dachi*)—Saifa, Seiunchin, Shisochin, Sepai, Sesan, and Kururunfa—or which katas begin with repetitions of three identical techniques—Saifa, Seiunchin, Shisochin, Sanseiru, Sesan, and Suparimpei. Much has been made of this sort of individual technique analysis.[2] But to suggest that certain katas are unrelated or have a different origin based on a "cluster analysis" of techniques depends largely on what data one inputs into the analysis or the parameters one sets, not to mention the size of the sample or the limited number of techniques one has chosen to analyze. While a focus on some techniques might imply that the Sanseiru and Sepai katas derive from different origins—one begins with a repetition of three techniques and the other doesn't—the similarity of the double-handed techniques illustrated below, for example, would seem to argue for a common source or at the very least that they are indeed forms from the same system (see illustrations 3A and 3B on page 33). Furthermore, to argue differences to support a theory that the original system taught by Higaonna Kanryo was comprised only of Sanchin, Sesan, Sanseiru, and Suparimpei katas seems purely academic; that is, it doesn't seem to get one's practice very far, unless, of course, there is a less than obvious political agenda for such an assertion. While this is not to discount the rather nebulous feeling that Kururunfa exhibits more affinity to Sepai and Saifa than it does to either Sesan or Sanseiru, there may be any number of explanations. Since there is really no definitive way to know the origins of any of the Goju-Ryu classical katas, or the myth-shrouded origins of any Chinese-based forms for that matter, it would seem to me to be a better use of one's time and effort to focus on similarities in techniques of the generally accepted canon of Goju-Ryu katas.

Variations on a Theme

When we compare the similarities between techniques in the different Goju-Ryu katas, what we see are *variations on a theme*. In looking at katas in this way, we start to see each of the katas as a part of a system—that is, related. We can then begin to examine the variations and question when it might be preferable to use one variation rather than another. We can also begin to examine the principles that different variations have in common. This is really the essence of kata study' and should be the focus of any study of a particular martial art. So often, students see an art as an infinite collection of techniques, as if we are meant to draw from this collection in the split-second of a life-threatening encounter. Those who advocate this sort of collection theory, or encyclopedic use of katas, argue that one simply needs to practice more if this seems overwhelming. This only serves to highlight the oft-repeated dojo admonition that one needs to practice a kata at least a thousand times before one understands it.

But this is, perhaps, a misunderstanding of what it means to practice. While there is certainly some truth to the idea that we practice so that our responses become second-nature, more importantly we practice in order to understand the principles behind the seemingly infinite variety of techniques. The system, then, becomes much more manageable. We begin to see not only how the system is put together, but also how we can effectively use it as a system of self-defense, and not merely resort to the same two or three techniques that we so often see in tournament sparring matches. For example:

We start to see (and feel) similarities between the opening move of Sepai kata and the "hammer-fist strike" in Saifa kata (see illustrations, 1A Sepai & 1B Saifa).

Or, we begin to see a similarity between the closed-hand two-handed blocking technique of Seiunchin kata and the open-hand double-hand blocks of Saifa (see illustration-2A Seiunchin & 2B Saifa).

Or, we notice that the two-handed technique from Sepai kata is very similar to the two-handed technique from Sanseiru kata (see illustrations 3A Sepai & 3B Sanseiru).

Or, we start to feel that the entry technique in the leaning-away stance followed by the front kick in Sepai kata (the beginning of the second sequence) is very much like the high-low horse stance blocking position in Seiunchin kata (see illustrations 4A Sepai & 4B Seiunchin).

Or, we notice that the grab and finger thrust (*nukite*) from Suparimpei looks the same as the grab and open hand technique from Seiunchin except one is in basic stance (*sanchin dachi*) and the other is done in horse stance (*shiko dachi*) (see illustrations Suparimpei 5A & Seiunchin 5B).

The question is: What does one do with the system once one begins to see the similarities between apparently different techniques from different katas? Might this simply be a case of redundancy? In the first example cited above (the opening move of Sepai kata and the hammer-fist strike from Saifa kata, see illustrations 1A & 1B), the techniques that follow also exhibit a certain similarity. One (Saifa) is followed by a closed-hand undercut punch, while the other (Sepai) is followed by an open hand coming under to the opponent's chin (see illustrations 6A & 6B).

However, even though they are similar, they are not the same; they each illustrate different responses depending on the circumstances of the attack or what follows. But, this similarity is the whole point of variations. Since the Saifa and Sepai sequences begin with the same "block" or receiving technique—and the techniques that follow also show a degree of similarity—one might continue the response initiated by the Saifa block and hammer-fist strike with the open hand to the chin, followed by the neck twist, of Sepai kata (see illustrations 7A thru 7D).

Alternatively, one might begin by "receiving" (*uke*) the opponent with the opening technique from Sepai kata—blocking with the left hand and striking with a downward knife-edge, while stepping back into horse stance (*shiko-dachi*). From here, one could continue moving into the controlling technique of this sequence from Sepai kata (see illustrations above, 7B and 7D) or, depending on how the opponent moves, tack on the finishing technique of Seiunchin kata (see illustrations 8B thru 8E).

If the opponent begins to stand up, for whatever reason, one can change to the knee kicks which open Kururunfa kata (see illustrations 9A–9B–9C).

Or, if the opponent begins to move in, one might step back and continue with the throw from Sepai kata (see illustrations 10A–10B–10C). Each of these is just an example to illustrate the way one can employ kata variations.

What quickly becomes apparent is that each kata within this "system" is composed of combinations or sequences (Hopkins, 2002). Some, of course, have argued that there is no way one can be sure that this is correct. I would be the first to admit that not all systems of traditional Asian martial arts seem to have preserved their forms with the same intent—showing application combinations. Some systems seem much more guarded, in a way, showing only techniques, like basics, that must be accompanied by the explanations of a knowledgeable teacher. And, of course, we don't have anyone around who was there at the beginning to ask. But neither did Copernicus or Galileo or Darwin. Scientific inquiry demands that we find other proof, and I would suggest three "proofs:" one, the techniques within the katas are self-referential, meaning they show variations within the larger system; two, when looked at in this way, the techniques are more deadly (effective), which is, of course, the whole point of a martial art; and three, in application, there is no disengagement from the opponent, reinforcing the Okinawan concept of sticking (*muchimi*) or *ippon kumite*—that is, allowing the opponent only one attack—and consequently more realistic.[3]

If we accept this initial premise then—that the Goju-Ryu katas are composed of combinations or sequences of techniques—it is easy to see that each combination can be broken down into entering or receiving techniques, bridging or controlling techniques, and finishing techniques.

The entry or receiving (*uke*) techniques depend on a variety of factors: the position of the defender, the speed and angle of the attack, and the direction of the attack, for example (see illustrations of opening or entry techniques, 11A thru 11J).

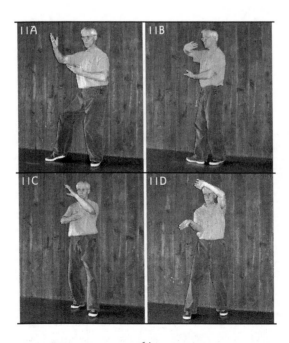

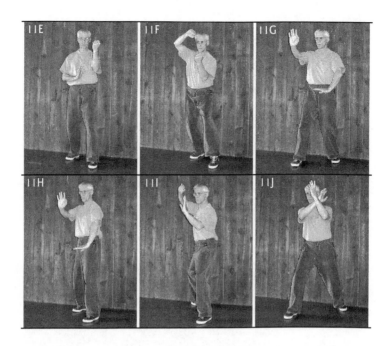

Examples of Opening or Entry Techniques

Each sequence begins with a block or receiving (*uke*) technique and generally an attack. Off-line movement or stepping accompanies each entry technique. There are a finite number of entry techniques (though more than are depicted here). The greater percentage of techniques in the Goju-Ryu classical katas is comprised of finishing techniques.

The receiving techniques (*uke*) of Goju-Ryu are almost always accompanied by a nearly simultaneous attack with the other hand, and generally to the opponent's head or neck. This can be seen in the final block and attack of Saifa kata, for instance (see illustration 11A). The defender is responding to a right punch, blocking with the left hand or forearm, and attacking the opponent's left-side head (or outside) with the right open hand.

Alternatively, in the final sequence of the Sepai kata, the defender is also responding to a right punch, blocking again with the left hand or forearm, but in this case attacking the opponent's right-side head or neck (or inside) with the right open hand (see illustration 11B). This technique is very similar to the opening technique of the Kururunfa kata—both attack the opponent's neck (inside) on the same side as the blocked attack (see illustration 11C).

The entry or receiving techniques then dictate to a large degree what necessarily follows—that is, the controlling and finishing techniques. If one begins with this last entry technique from Saifa kata (illustration 11A)—though one may, of course, continue with the same sequence that is shown in the kata,[4] one might also change the response to any of the techniques in any of the other kata that also begin with a block and opposite-side head attack. For example, one might shift into the kicking sequence of Saifa and stay within the same kata (see illustrations 12A–12B–12C), or one might draw the head down and attack to the back of the neck as in Suparimpei kata (see illustrations 12A–13B–13C).

One might even turn to face the attacker, step back into a right-foot-forward cat stance (*neko-ashi-dachi*), grab the head, and use the knee to attack the opponent's face, as in Seiunchin kata (see illustrations 12A–14B–14C). The variations—or how and when one changes from one sequence of techniques to another—are dictated by the opponent's responses and the ever-changing circumstances of a self-defense scenario.

This is particularly true of the bridging or controlling techniques—techniques that generally involve grasping or holding the opponent—that depend largely on the response of the attacker to the defender's initial move. There are any number of different controlling and finishing techniques. So, what we see as possible responses in a situation actually multiply. One could, for instance, begin with the receiving or entry technique from the Sepai kata and tack on the controlling and finishing techniques from the Saifa kata, or vice-versa, as in the illustration above. It all depends on how fluent or practiced one is with the whole system. Or one might continue from the Sepai opening technique (a block and nearly simultaneous attack to the back of the opponent's neck) to the controlling and finishing techniques found in a later sequence from the Sepai kata (see illustrations 15A–15B–15C).

There are, after all, only a limited number of ways to receive (*uke*) or block an opponent's attack. But once one has "blocked" or intercepted the opponent's attack, there is a wide range of controlling techniques or finishing techniques to draw from. And at any point in the sequence one might move between the techniques of different katas. The variations seem to branch out almost like a spider web. It's analogous to a jazz musician who practices scales and familiar melodies endlessly, so that he or she can seem to "improvise" effortlessly.

It should be emphasized here that one changes in response to the opponent's movements; one doesn't merely disengage and start over again, trying something else, if the initial response doesn't work. After one receives or blocks the opponent's initial attack, the idea is to adhere or stick to the opponent, following his movement, as one counterattacks.

Any one kata then, it might be assumed, shows only one possible scenario out of many. Other katas show variations or, in other words, other possible scenarios. (Of course, these themes and variations are shown within the same kata as well.) One might, in fact, go further along these lines and suggest what may seem blasphemous to some: that katas are not, in one sense at least, sacrosanct. This is not to suggest that the katas themselves should be changed, but that in practicing, in seeking to understand katas, one should be able to disconnect techniques within the katas and reconnect them in different ways. This sort of exploration gives one the flexibility to apply the kata techniques in response to self-defense situations that are fluid and changing. For example: one might respond to an attacker's push by moving diagonally, blocking with both hands, as done in Saifa, and kicking. But instead of stepping up and using the second knee or kick, as in a continuation of this sequence in Saifa, one might step back, drawing the head down, and use the forearm to attack the opponent's neck, as in Seiunchin kata (see illustrations 16A thru 16D).

Or, one might begin with the double-handed entry technique from Sanseiru, and then step around and throw the attacker as one does in Sepai kata (see illustrations 17A thru 17D).

Listening Points

In these illustrations, the defender is initially responding with the entry technique at the beginning of the Kururunfa kata (18A). The initial block and entry can then easily change into a host of controlling and finishing techniques taken from other katas: the continuation of the initial sequence in the Kururunfa kata (18B–C); next, Shisochin kata (18D–E); the final technique from the Suparimpei kata (18F–G); and the ending of the Sepai kata (18H–I).

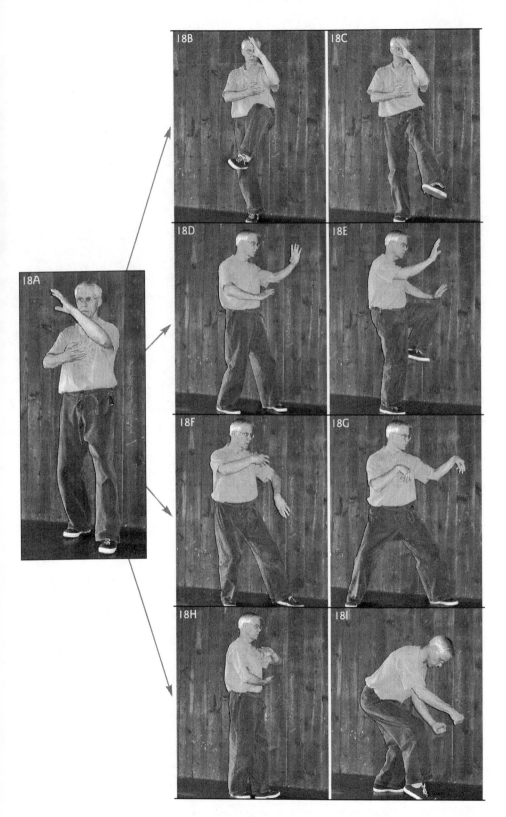

Listening Points

Changing one's response to an attack or when to employ variations generally occurs at the point of contact with the opponent's attack. The initial blocking position of the hands occurs in a number of places in different katas, but at the point of initial contact the defender's movement is incomplete. The hand position here (19A) is showing the point at which the defender's hands contact the hands of the attacker.

It is at this point of contact that the defender "listens" to the attack and responds appropriately. This is the point at which one might change to any of the entry techniques illustrated from various katas (19B, or 19C, or 19D, or 19E) .

Left: Matayoshi showing author scrolls at his home in 1986.
Right: Matayoshi, with some of the author's senior students, visiting the author's dojo in 1995. Brush script by Matayoshi of "kokoro" (spirit) displayed in the author's dojo.

What I am suggesting is another, perhaps new, way of training: studying katas and their applications (*bunkai*), not individually but in their relationship to other katas and similar applications. It's also a way of training what the Chinese martial arts refer to as sensitivity—being able to instantaneously change one's technique in response to the opponent's movements. We take, for instance, one entry technique (usually a "block" or *uke* and simultaneous attack with the other hand) and see where we can go from there, how many variations we can tack on to the end of it. In the process, we move sometimes within the same kata—because katas have themes— and sometimes between similar techniques in other katas, but we learn and begin to use a system of self-defense as it was meant to be used.

Conclusion

It is difficult to argue that the different Goju-Ryu katas come from independent sources or the polyglot nature of a system that seems to be so self-referential. There is a lot of argument nowadays that Miyagi Chojun either created many katas of his own or brought them back from China, but that in any case these katas— Saifa, Seiunchin, Shishochin, Sepai, Kururunfa among them—were not part of the original system taught by Higaonna Kanryo. This theory suggests that these katas have a separate origin, distinct and perhaps unrelated to the origins of Sanchin, Sanseiru, Sesan, and Suparimpei. I would suggest, however, the very fact that techniques seem to reference other techniques in other katas—that is, they appear to be variations on a theme, if you will, we should accept the Goju canon as it has been passed down, as a system—and it is the whole Goju-Ryu system that one must be conversant with in order to employ the katas' techniques in the way that they were originally intended, not merely one or two or even three katas.[5] It is an oft-repeated story that in the old days teachers like Miyagi Chojun taught Sanchin kata and only one or two other katas to each student, depending on the student's ability or body type. From this, authors Lawrence Kane and Kris Wilder conclude that "each kata contains a complete, integrated fighting system." In fact, they go a step further to suggest that in modern times, when each "practitioner is given a lot more material to digest"—all eight classical subjects of the Goju-Ryu canon, for instance—"it is quite understandable for their level of comprehension to be somewhat less" (Kane & Wilder, 2005: 21). But we don't want to extrapolate from legend—we know that there were many that learned the whole system, all the katas. And we should recognize that any one kata is not complete in itself, nor should we necessarily have a favorite kata. There is no playing of favorites; one must invest in the whole system.

I am reminded of something that Matayoshi once said that summer so long ago. One evening, he invited us to his house for dinner. After dinner, he started to show us different examples of calligraphy, taking them down from a shelf where he had

73

them stored away and spreading them out on the floor. Some were wonderful scrolls of the *Goju Happo* (Eight Laws), some were charts of lineage, others were single character sayings. Many of them had been given to him as presents. One was a particularly beautiful example of free-form brush work (*sosho* or grass writing). This one was the kanji script for "*kokoro*," or spirit, though that is perhaps a rather limited translation. In any case, Matayoshi took out a brush and wrote his name on the side, stamped it with his seal, and handed it to me. He stressed the importance of spirit in training, and that the exercise of karate trained not just the body but the spirit as well.

Many of these lessons, of course, come to mind when I enter the dojo and see this piece of calligraphy hanging on the wall. It also reminds me of what George Donahue talks about in his article, "Kata, Bunkai and Calligraphy"—how kata may start off at the beginner stage, like calligraphy, stiff and formal, but that over time, it becomes more fluid, like the "grass writing" of Japanese calligraphy. I once sat in on a writing class on a visit to a Japanese high school in Hokkaido, the northern most province of Japan, a long way from Okinawa. We spent an enjoyable hour laughing and practicing calligraphy alongside a class full of giggling high schoolers, filling in large-squared graph paper with basic brush strokes. Each of 10,000 or so pictographic characters is made up of only a very few different strokes—they're just

arranged differently on the paper. To me, this is like katas. If one understands the system as a whole, one can take the techniques, or characters, apart and rearrange them in different combinations until one's self-defense is fluid, changing, and almost limitless. The only thing that may prevent us from discovering these themes and variations within katas is a rigid and ritualistic adherence to mindless regimentation. Perhaps as Matayoshi often suggested—and as my own teacher, Kimo Wall, passed on to me, after a rigorous training session, where each technique in the katas was corrected and perfected, we would be well advised to tell our students to "go play."

Kimo Wall and Gibo Seki in Japan, 1986.

Notes

[1] Many of the teachers who studied under Miyagi Chojun have formed different schools or branches of Goju-Ryu (Higa Seko's Shodokan, Yagi Meitoku's Meibukan, Toguchi Seikichi's Shoreikan, Miyazato Ei'ichi's Jundokan) and there

are often slight or not-so-slight differences in katas. Gibo Seki is a senior teacher in the Shodokan.

[2] See F. Camara and M. McKenna, who have suggested that a "cluster analysis" of techniques within the Goju-Ryu kata may "prove" that there are really two strains or sources of the katas that form the Goju-Ryu system: one group that Higaonna taught, comprised of Sanchin, Sanseiru, Sesan, and Suparimpei; and the other group added to the system by Miyagi, comprised of Saifa, Seiunchin, Shisochin, Sepai, Kururunfa, and Tensho. It may be worth noting here that even if the structure of various katas differ, implying a different kata origin, the techniques within the kata may not necessarily be from a different source. Also see M. Ravignat, elaborating on an earlier article by Charles Swift, who suggests that the katas that comprise the accepted Goju-Ryu canon were not all taught by Higaonna to Miyagi Chojun, but may have come from different sources. He bases his ideas on, among other things, a perception of symmetry and asymmetry in various katas—the Higaonna katas being asymmetrical and the Miyagi katas being symmetrical. But even the most superficial analysis would suggest that this may be an over-simplification.

[3] Dan Smith, a noted Shorin-Ryu teacher, has suggested that this idea of "one punch, one kill" has been misunderstood. Smith writes: "All Okinawan karate has the same objective and that is to stop an attack and survive without being hurt. We call this *ippon kumite* or one technique fighting. Many people think that ippon kumite is a promised fight that only allows one attack from the opponent, but this is not what the Okinawans intended. The meaning is that if you move out of the way and block effectively, the opponent will only have the chance to make one attack. Your counterattack follows the practice of only allowing one attack."

[4] To see the standard application for this last technique of Saifa kata, see article: Hopkins (2004).

[5] Compare to what Burgar sets out to do in his oft-cited book, *Five Years, One Kata*. While an admirable expression of perseverance, unless one is imaginative enough to find the rest of the system within a single kata, such a practice seems of little practical use, notwithstanding the Thoreau-like analogy: "I have traveled much in Concord."

Bibliography

Burgar, B. (2003). *Five years, one kata*. Hemel Hempstead, UK: Martial Arts Publishing.

Camara, F. & McKenna, M. (2007). A preliminary analysis of Goju-Ryu kata structure. *Journal of Asian Martial Arts, 16*(4), 46–53.

Donahue, G. (2003, April 1). Kata, bunkai & calligraphy. http://www.fightingarts.com/reading/article.php?id=154

Hopkins, G. (2002). The lost secrets of Goju-Ryu: What the kata shows. *Journal of Asian Martial Arts, 11*(4), 54–77.

Hopkins, G. (2004). The shape of kata: An enigma of pattern. *Journal of Asian Martial Arts, 13*(1), 64–77.

Kane, L., & Wilder, K. (2005). *The way of kata: a comprehensive guide to deciphering martial applications*. Boston: YMAA Publication Center.

Ravignat, M. (2004). The history of Goju-Ryu karate: New ideas on Goju-Ryu's direct Chinese ancestors. www. Meibukanmagazine.org

Smith, D. (2002). From a private correspondence, March 10, 2002.

Swift, C. (2003). The kenpo of Kume village. *Dragon* Times, (23): 10–12 and 34.

Acknowledgements

A special thanks to my students, Bill and Lucas Diggle, for demonstrating applications. Also, thanks to my wife, Martha, for her editorial assistance and patience, and the teachers who have helped me along the way: Kimo Wall, Matayoshi Shinpo, and Gibo Seki. Comments on the article can be sent to Email: Kodokan3@msn.com

Glossary		Katas	
Bunkai	分解	Kururunfa	久留頓破
Chi shi	力石	Saifa	砕破
Goju-ryu	剛柔流	Sanchin	三戦
Higa Seiko	比嘉 世幸	Sanseiru	三十六(手)
Higashionna Kanryo	東恩納 寛量	Seipai	十八(手)
Jundokan	順道館	Seisan	十三(手)
Kata	型, 形	Seiunchin	制引戦
Kingai-ryu	金硬流	Shisochin	四向戦
Kobudo	古武道	Suparinpei	壱百零八
Meibukan	明武館	Tensho	転掌
Miyagi Chojun	宮城 長順		
Miyazato Ei'ichi	榮一宮里		
Nigiri game	にぎりがめ		
Shodokan	尚道館		
Shoreikan	昭霊館		
Shorin-ryu	小林流		
Yagi Meitoku	明德八木		

Nahate:
The Old-School Okinawan Martial Art and Its Original Four-Kata Curriculum, Part I

by Mario McKenna, M.S.

Above:
Photograph of Higaonna Kanryo (1850–1915).

Left:
Karate practice at Shuri Castle, c. 1938.

Nahate

Nahate (那覇手), along with Shurite and Tomarite, was an important boxing culture practiced in and around the Kumemura area of Naha (Kumemura, Wikipedia), Okinawa. For several generations it was passed down until the late nineteenth century, when its popularity began to wane. Its resurgence is most often ascribed to Higaonna Kanryo (1850–1915). Folklore tells us that Higaonna traveled to Fuzhou city in China's Fujian province and remained there for up to fifteen years, studying Chinese boxing from a teacher called Ryu Ryu Ko (aka., Ru Ru Ko, 1852–1930). Who Ryu Ryu Ko was and what he taught Higaonna is a point of debate among karate historians that has yet to be satisfactorily resolved (Kinjo, 1999; Tokashiki, 1991).

Be that as it may, Higaonna eventually returned to Okinawa and began teaching his system to a small group of students in Naha. Orthodox history states that he taught nine katas: Sanchin, Saifa, Seiunchin, Sanseru, Sepai, Shisochin, Sesan, Kururunfa, and Suparimpei/Pechurin, which were then passed down by his most prolific student, and founder of Goju-Ryu, Miyagi Chojun (1888–1952).

However, my own contention is that the original Nahate curriculum consisted of four katas: Sanchin, Sesan, Sanseru, and Suparimpei/Pechurin (Câmara & McKenna, 2007; McKenna & Swift, 2002; McKenna, 2001; McKenna, 2000a, 2000b).

That said, I would like to discuss the content of these four Nahate katas—Sanchin, Sesan, Sanseru, and Suparimpei/Pechurin—in more detail in order to provide the reader with a better understanding of the rich techniques each of them contains. To do this, I will compare and contrast the two major lineages of Nahate with respect to these kata that originated from Higaonna Kanryo: Goju-Ryu (剛柔流) and Tou'on-Ryu (東恩流). Throughout these essays I will briefly explain the main techniques found in each kata and their applications, along with some of the verbal explanations that descended with these traditions, and finally the importance of hidden meaning in katas.

三戦 Sanchin Kata

The Sanchin kata forms the basis for Nahate techniques. Although there are many superficially different versions of this kata, essentially all of them can trace their origin to Higaonna Kanryo, or, to a lesser extent, Uechi Kanbun.[1] Regardless of the version practiced, the technical content of the kata is largely the same:

1) stance,   2) midlevel blocks and thrusts,
3) turning,   4) grasping hands and fingertip thrusts, and
5) the circle block.

Let's examine each of these parts one by one.

1. Stance.

2a. Sanchin midlevel block/punch, Goju.
2b. Sanchin midlevel block/punch, Tou'on.

---

[1] There are other variations that exist (e.g., Okinawa Kenpo, Motobu-ryu, etc.), but these are minor katas and will not be considered for the purpose of this article, as they follow essentially the same form and have the same technical content.

3) Sanchin turn.
4) Sanchin double spear hand thrust.

5a) Sanchin circle block, Goju.
5b) Sanchin circle block, Tou'on.

Sanchin Kata and Combative Concepts

When two people face each other during a modern, sport free-fighting exchange, they will start at quite a distance from each other. As a result, the percentage of strikes that land is quite low, and those that do land are not target specific. In general, we could say that modern free-fighting practice tends to be inaccurate in its strikes. We can also observe that the striking distance is closed quite rapidly—only after a few strikes have been exchanged.

When we contrast this method to the older Nahate practices and techniques as embodied in the Sanchin kata, we can see some very interesting differences: A) the engagement distance (*maai*) is much closer; B) body position, alignment, and placement are extremely important; C) seizing (*tuidi*), locking (*chigedi*), and entangling (*karamidi*) techniques followed by strikes dominate.

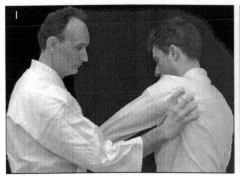

1) Seizing.   2) Locking.

3) Entangling.

These types of techniques have a number of advantages, two of which are increased precision and power when striking. Nahate's seizing, locking, and entangling techniques secure an opponent, which allows a greater possibility of striking smaller and potentially more effective targets with greater accuracy and with more effective tools (e.g., one-knuckle fist [*ippon ken*]). These are techniques you would never see used in a free-fighting exchange because they are quite literally too dangerous. Therefore, when we think about the training methods used in the past, we should consider them not as methods of fighting per se, but as methods of self-protection.

Sanchin Stance

At the heart of the Sanchin kata is the Sanchin stance. According to Hirakami Nobuyuki, this stance is very rare in mainland Japanese martial culture, with the possible exception of old-style sumo (Hirakami, 2000). Indeed, Sanchin stance appears unique to Okinawan martial culture and emphasizes a natural posture with the weight evenly distributed on both legs with the toes of the lead foot slightly turned to the inside. The importance of Sanchin stance is in teaching the student how to generate, store, and release energy when striking. This explosive type of energy is commonly referred to as *fajing* in Chinese martial culture (發勁; Japanese: *hakkei*). Therefore, we can think of Sanchin stance as allowing for the efficient transfer of energy generated by the body and delivered through the arms.

Midlevel Block and Thrust

Sanchin's midlevel block is performed on the same side as the lead leg. In contrast, the punch is delivered with the opposite hand of the lead leg, and is therefore commonly referred to as a reverse punch (*gyaku tsuki*). There are a few minor differences between Tou'on-Ryu and Goju-Ryu with respect to these techniques. The two most noticeable ones are chambering the fist at the chest versus the hip, and thrusting straight out versus to the centerline. Putting aside these differences for the moment, the most common applications of these techniques are to deflect an incoming strike (either to the inside or outside) and to counter with a punch to the opponent's body. Although acceptable for teaching beginning students, this is a very crude explanation of this technique and grossly simplifies many of its deeper applications, which include the aforementioned seizing, grabbing, and locking techniques.

Not only do these sorts of rudimentary explanations obfuscate many of the more jujutsu-like applications found in Sanchin and in other katas, but they also create the idea that kata techniques cannot be used in an actual confrontation (which, ironically, is often described in the context of modern sport competition, such as sport karate, mixed martial arts, wrestling, or boxing). Some modern karate styles have attempted to overcome this perceived weakness by creating various forms of arranged sparring, such as one-step or three-step sparring, but these methods are modern creations, with the oldest known being published by Funakoshi Gichin (1868–1957) in *The Karatedo Instruction Book* (*Karatedo Kyohan*). Furthermore, they are largely divorced from actual kata technique. The solution is that function does not always follow form in old karate (Okinawan: *toudi*) katas (Hirakami, 2000).

As I mentioned earlier, when we think about the combination of Sanchin stance, midlevel block, and reverse punch, we see it is never used in modern, sport-based karate competition. In contrast, lunging forward stances and reverse punches between contestants who are meters apart are more commonly seen. Why is it we do not see the former? The answer is surprisingly simple: because that technique is far too dangerous to be used in competition. It is quite literally meant to destroy the attacker (Hirakami, 2000). One simple example of its use in downing an attacker is to use entangling techniques (*karamidi*), in which the "blocking" arm wraps the opponent's arm and the reverse punch is used to attack the centerline.[2] This technique would lead to disqualification in a tournament, but when used as a self-protection method, it is clearly an effective and powerful technique.

Left: Sanchin midlevel block and punch.

Right: Sanchin entangled arm.

Fingertip Thrust and Grasping Hands

Near the end of the Sanchin kata there are three clenching pulls and three open-hand fingertip thrusts. These are essentially performed the same in Goju-Ryu and Tou'on-Ryu. The full sequence consists of grasping with both hands, closing them into fists, and pulling them back to the waist or chest, followed by opening the hands, turning them over, and thrusting with the fingertips. Let's examine the use of the fingertip thrusts by looking at a historical example.

In *An Overview of Karatedo* (1938), Shiroma Shimpan describes the formation and use of fingertip thrusts in his chapter called "Karatedo Kata and Their Meaning." Shiroma first describes the technique: "If the back of the hand is facing upwards and the fingers are held horizontally then it is known as horizontal fingertip thrusts [*sic*]. Horizontal fingertip thrusts can be seen in the kata Sanchin. In Sanchin kata both hands are held at midlevel and simultaneously strike using horizontal fingertip thrusts" (Nakasone, 2009: 97).

---

[2] This same technique is overtly shown in the Uechi-ryu kata Sanseru, but in place of a regular fist, a one-knuckle fist is used.

Sanchin finger tip strike to the throat.

Shiroma (Nakasone, 2009: 98) explains the use of this technique:

If an opponent fixes his eyes on your solar plexus and launches an attack, we use the principle of simultaneous attack and defense as I have previously explained by using double horizontal fingertip thrusts to both attack and defend. This double sided fingertip thrusts [sic] is a very effective technique. If however, the opponent strikes at your face you can perform an open hand side block and with the same hand you can strike your opponent's face with either horizontal or vertical fingertip thrusts. Therefore high and midlevel fingertip thrusts are both an effective and advantageous means of attack and defense.

Circle Block

The final sequence of Sanchin kata in both Goju-Ryu and Tou'on-Ryu consists of stepping back one step in Sanchin stance and performing a circle block. In Goju-Ryu it is referred to as "circle block" (*mawashi uke*), while in Tou'on-Ryu it is referred to as "comma block" (*tomoe uke*). There is a noticeable difference how the block is performed between the sister styles, but we will get to this important difference a little bit later.

The circle block is an extremely powerful technique that is often applied as a strike. This is a completely valid application of the technique, but it expresses only one dimension of it. An alternate name for this technique is *tora guchi*—the mouth of the tiger. The choice of name is quite interesting, as it evokes the frightening image of a tiger consuming its prey. But why this name? As you are probably aware, there are superficial (*omote*) and deeper (*ura*) applications of techniques in karate (*toudi*), and this includes the circle block. In this light, the striking application can be seen as a superficial application, but a deeper application would be the use of tora guchi in some other manner.

I think most people who practice Sanchin have thought of this and may even have stumbled onto a few alternative uses for tora guchi during their practices, but I would encourage you to continue to delve deeper into its study. There are countless applications for tora guchi: locks, throws, sweeps, traps, etc. I suspect that if your background is sports-based karate, then these applications may not be readily apparent, but with a little effort and experimentation outside of a sports context, they will reveal themselves to you little by little. Of course, it helps if your teacher is knowledgeable with these techniques, but it is not essential—at least not in the beginning.

Now let's return to the differences between Tou'on-Ryu and Goju-Ryu and how they perform the circle block at the end of Sanchin kata. In it, the arms are not extended out to project energy as you would as if trying to strike (this is more apparent in the Uechi-Ryu interpretation and less so in the Goju-Ryu version but still present). Instead the arms (especially the elbows) are kept close to the body. Also the position of the palms is quite different, with the upper hand in front of the collarbone and the lower hand in front of the groin. From this position one can easily "devour" an opponent. In closing I will leave the reader with the following image to contemplate the meaning of the circle block: "[T]he tiger always catches its prey" (Hirakami, 2000: pt. VI, 63).

Psychological Aspects to Sanchin

Not only does Sanchin kata provide deep technical and physical training; it also provides profound training for the spirit and mind. This is expressed very eloquently by Dr. Takamiyagi Shigeru, a high-ranking Uechi-Ryu teacher of the Okikukai (Okinawan Karatedo Association) in his essay entitled "Sanchin and its Five Cardinal Points" (Takamiyagi, 1996: 158).

> The practice of Sanchin, the foundation kata of Okikukai, develops the student in five ways that reach beyond the basic needs of exercise or self-defense. Properly understood, Sanchin is a philosophical statement. The five benefits of Sanchin are as follows:
> 1) Sanchin integrates all parts of the stance;
> 2) Sanchin corrects the breathing;
> 3) Sanchin develops penetrating eyes;
> 4) Sanchin cultivates spiritual concentration;
> 5) Sanchin strengthens the body.
> The key for understanding Sanchin is "integration." Proper stance anchors the student to the floor; while proper concentration and breathing integrates all body movements. Proper eye contact demonstrates uninterrupted awareness, focusing the mind on every area of attack of the opponent. To develop a strong and integrated Sanchin kata is to forge a well-honed and ordered self.

Comments on Sanchin

There are a few expressions that have been passed down in karate (toudi) about the importance of Sanchin kata, such as, "Sanchin is the beginning and the end," or, "Three years of study for Sanchin kata." These expressions tell us that although a short kata, Sanchin formed the backbone of Nahate upon which subsequent technique and understanding were built. In the next part of this chapter I will discuss the Sesan kata.

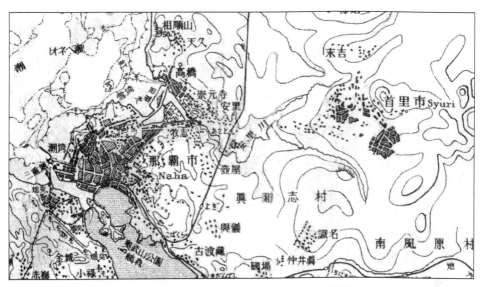

Detail from a 1937 nautical chart showing the area around Naha city. Naha to Shuri (Syuri) is about three miles. *From the Library of Congress print collection.*

十三手 Sesan Kata

The next kata in the Nahate curriculum we will discuss is Sesan, which is typically viewed as an intermediate-level kata.[3] Sesan is written as the number "13" but the reason for this is not entirely clear. Some teachers have stated that Sesan refers to the number of individual or composite techniques in the kata, while others state that it refers to the number of steps in the kata. For some, these methods sum to thirteen, leading them to believe that this is the meaning of Sesan (see Tokashiki, 1991; Kinjo, 1999). However, overall these methods of defining Sesan are unsatisfactory because of their inconsistency when applied across the different lineages of Sesan found in karate (toudi). What we can say with some certainty is that Sesan builds upon the techniques learned from Sanchin.

---

[3] Interestingly enough, in Tou'on-Ryu and Uechi-Ryu, Sesan is taught before Sanseru.

For this portion, I will only be examining the Sesan taught by Higaonna Kanryo (1850–1915), which, unfortunately, was not passed down in Tou'on-Ryu. Therefore a cross-comparison within the same lineage of kata cannot be done. Tou'on-Ryu uses a version of Sesan, which originates from Higaonna Kanyu (1849–1922) and differs quite markedly in comparison to the Kanryo version. With that said, let's take a look at some of the techniques found in the Higaonna Kanryo version of Sesan.

Sword-Hand Strike and Continuous Block

Like Sanchin kata, Sesan opens with three steps forward in Sanchin stance in conjunction with three midlevel blocks and punches. As this was already discussed in the Sanchin section, I'll move on to the next major set of techniques: a sword-hand strike followed by three rapid blocks and three double fingertip thrusts and knee strikes in succession.

First, let's examine the continuous block. These are unique to Sesan kata and are a solid example of a practical self-defense technique. They are excellent for a number of reasons, but let's highlight two of them. First, they are executed toward the centerline of the opponent's body while simultaneously protecting your own, and second, they can be used to deflect an attack and simultaneously counter toward vulnerable parts of the throat and head. This series of blocks is referred to as *renzoku uke* in Japanese and is described in *An Outline of Karatedo* by Shiroma Shimpan in his chapter called "Karate Kata and their Meaning" (Nakasone, 1938: 104):

> When your opponent punches with his right fist, you block his attack with your left forearm (the right forearm is then held ready). However if your opponent attacks again with his left fist, you can quickly raise your right forearm to block his attack. [This technique is illustrated in figures 1 and 2.] Renzoku-uke is intended to block multiple strikes from an opponent, but during an actual fight it is not enough to simply block the attack; this is meaningless. It is vital to quickly strike your opponent's oncoming blow with your right or left hand chambered in front of you (since in karatedo kata double or triple punches are executed).

> When shifting from defense to offense with renzoku-uke, either in kata or in actual fighting, a useful technique is nukite . . . . For example, after executing the third renzoku-uke you can strike your opponent with a right tate nukite (or *yoko nukite*). Even if your opponent simultaneously punches at you with his right fist, you will have the advantage because your right hand is on the inside.

1) Shiroma Renzoku Uke.
2) Shiroma Renzoku Uke Applied.

Low-Level Side Kick and Turn

In Sanchin kata there are no kicks, but in Sesan the first kick a student learns through this kata is the low-level side kick. This kick is typically taught to attack the opponent's knee and is an adequate (albeit limited) explanation of its application. Other applications can include sweeps to the front or back of the knee or ankle, and are dangerous. In addition, the turn in Sesan can be used to throw an opponent. The Sesan rendition is to prop the opponent's foot and use the turn to trip him—an exceedingly simple technique, and one that is more reminiscent of jujutsu than modern judo (Hirakami, 2000).

These kinds of simple sweeps can be found in Takenouchi-ryu jujutsu and are well suited to real combat, as they allow the defender to maintain a stable position while being able to throw an opponent to the ground with minimal effort (Hirakami, 2000). Unfortunately, in some modern dojos, practice takes place on hard floors, making it difficult to use such techniques safely. As a result, the low-level side kick is usually literally applied as a kick to the knee as described earlier. Even more discouraging is that the practice of these kinds of throwing techniques has mostly disappeared in modern karate training.

Sesan low-level
side kick, applied.

Scooping Block

The next section of Sesan introduces a new technique, the scooping block, which resembles open-hand mid- and low-level blocks. A typical application of the scooping block is to deflect an opponent's attack with one hand, and hook and pull as the other hand strikes the face. This is a surface-level application and is adequate for beginning students, but intermediate students should be thinking of deeper applications. To give you an example of a deeper meaning of scooping block, Tou'on-Ryu students are taught that this technique can be an entangling technique (karamidi), and they should think along these lines when applying the technique to an opponent. For example, using the block's low-level portion to deflect and seize an attack, and the midlevel portion of the block to entangle the opponent's arm at the elbow and force him down.

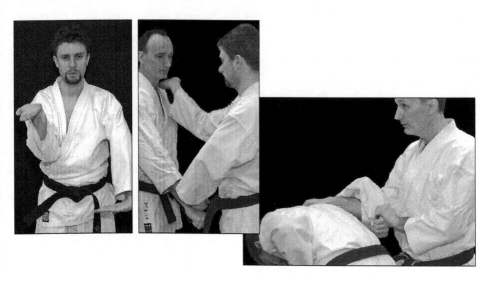

Sesan scoop block and applications.

Combination Punches and Low Side Kick

The next main technique sequence that we'll look at is the combination punches found in Sesan that are performed to the right and left.[4] After blocking the opponent's attack, the defender enters and strikes the opponent with a combination of punches. Although simple in appearance, this technique is very dynamic and powerful. This sort of aggressive punching technique is very rare in mainland Japanese jujutsu, and it is perhaps one reason why there might have been such a strong interest in karate (toudi) when it was demonstrated on Okinawa to judo founder Kano Jigoro, and later on the Japanese mainland at the Kodokan. Be that as it may, the combination punch in Sesan is a simple but elegant technique intended to down an opponent quickly.

The first series of punches consists of a vertical-fist punch followed by two rapid twisting punches. The vertical-fist punch is very important, as it introduces the concept of short power (*chinkuchi*). This image may draw to mind the idea of a "one-inch punch" delivered in Bruce Lee's style (Jeet Kune Do), but instead the idea is to generate maximal force in a swift and relatively short distance. This requires a strong base, which should have been previously developed when practicing Sanchin kata—relaxing the shoulders, elbows in, coordination of the breath, and continuity of reaction forces from the ground through the leg, hips, back, arms, and into the target. This is one reason we traditionally see the progression of the kata as Sanchin to Sesan. After the vertical-fist punch, the two twisting punches are delivered, followed by a low-level block and low-level side kick. We have already discussed this type of punch in the section on Sanchin kata.

Sesan vertical fist.

The next punching sequence is three twisting punches performed to the opposite side. Before we discuss this sequence, let's spend a few moments looking at the movement just before the punches. It consists of sliding forward, dropping into a horse stance, and performing a hooking block. A rather nice analogy for this technique is to think of a tiger pouncing on its prey and grasping it with its claws. With the attacker temporarily immobilized, three rapid-fire punches are delivered. The rhythm of these punches may vary, but they are all delivered with a heavy feel to them, and with a slight downward trajectory.

---

[4] Of note are the twisting combination punches that are only found in Sesan, and not seen in Sanchin, Sanseru, or Suparimpei/Pechurin. Likewise, they are also not found in Saifa, Seiunchin, Sepai, Shisochin, or Kururunfa.

Sesan hooking block and application.

Uppercut, Backfist, Dropping Elbow Strike, Low-Level Block, Hook Punch, and Low Side Kick

Following the combination punches is a long and complex sequence of techniques delivered in rapid succession. Most of these techniques are encountered in Sesan kata for the first time and introduce a novel set of tools to be learned and mastered. Although there are a bewildering number of uses of these techniques, we will just focus on a few of the less obvious ones to show their utility. The first one we will look at incorporates locking and throwing techniques and was popularized by the late Goju-Ryu Shoreikan founder, Toguchi Seikichi (1917–1998) (see, Toguchi, Wikipedia). It involves seizing the attacker's right arm, delivering the uppercut and backfist to the face, and then using the dropping elbow to lock and secure the arm. The low-level block is then used to prop the inside knee, and the attacker is rolled forward, somewhat like the judo throws *tomoenage* (circle throw) or *taniotoshi* (valley drop).

Above: Sesan throw.

Right: Sesan throw, entangled.

The next application we will look at is less spectacular, but perhaps a bit more practical, especially since it incorporates the idea of karamidi. Like the previous example, it starts with seizing the attacker's arm, but from the outside, and then delivering the uppercut and backfist strikes to the face. The dropping elbow strike is used to bend the attacker's arm at the elbow, while the low-level block strikes the groin and then encircles the attacker's arm to lock it. With the attacker secured, the hook punch delivers a strike to the face, and the low side kick is used to kick or throw the attacker to the ground.

Sesan backfist and entangled.

Front Kick and Reverse Punch

The next segment of Sesan we'll look at is the front kick and reverse punch combination. The front kick is the second kick introduced in Sesan after the low-level side kick. It is executed by seizing the opponent and kicking directly into his body. The next technique after the front kick is the reverse punch. Previously, this punch was taught using Sanchin stance, but now it is performed in a forward stance while the other hand simultaneously does a palm block. At face value, this technique is quite simple and brutally effective, but, as with other techniques, there are various levels to applying it.

Sesan applications:
1) sweeping block/strike,
2) palm-heel,
3) front kick.

Cat Stance and Circle Block

Sesan ends by performing a circle block from the cat stance. As I have already talked about the circle block, I won't discuss it here, but I will touch upon the importance of the cat stance. The cat stance provides the defender with a new protective strategy. In modern karate, it is typically explained as a fighting posture, but this runs counter to old-style karate (toudi), which does not use static postures (Nakasone, 1938: 86). Although there are many uses for the cat stance, in Sesan kata it is used in conjunction with a circle block. In this context, tora guchi is used to capture and ensnare (karamidi) the opponent's arms, and the cat stance is used to move the defender's center of gravity in order to drop the opponent to the ground. It also allows the quick delivery of a kick with the lead leg.

Left:
Sesan circle block application.

Right:
applied with leg sweep.

Acknowledgments

I would like to extend my sincerest thanks to Mr. Maik Hassel for taking the photographs that illustrate this article, and to Mr. Olivier Riche and Mr. Brent Zaparniuk for posing for the photographs.

Bibliography

Câmara, F. & McKenna, M. (2007). A preliminary analysis of Goju-Ryu kata structure. *Journal of Asian Martial Arts, 16* (4), 46–53.

Hirakami, N. (2001). Koden Ryukyu Kenpo: Nahate no Himitsu. *Gekkan Hiden:* Issues 1–10.

Kinjo, A. (1999). *Karate denshin roku.* Okinawa: Tosho Center.

Kumemura. http://en.wikipedia.org/wiki/Kumemura

McKenna, M. & Swift, C. (2002). Etmology of Goju Ryu kata. *Dragon Times:* 21: 12–13, 35.

McKenna, M. (2001). Chinese boxing master Go Ken Ki: Okinawan karate. *Dragon Times,* 20, 13–15.

McKenna, M. (2000a). To-on-ryu: A glimpse into karate-do's roots. *Journal of Asian Martial Arts,* 9 (3), 32–43.

McKenna, M. (2000b). Exploring Goju Ryu's past, part 1 & 2. *Dragon Times,* 19: 18–19; 15–17.

Nakasone, G. (2009). An *overview of karatedo*–English Translation and Commentary by Mario McKenna. Raleigh, N.C.: Lulu Press.

Takamiyagi, S. (1996). Sanchin and its five cardinal points (pg. 158). publisher?

Toguchi. http://en.wikipedia.org/wiki/Seikichi_Toguchi

Tokashiki, I. (1991). *Gohaku-kai nenkanshi.* Naha: Published privately.

Nahate:
The Old-School Okinawan Martial Art and Its Original Four-Kata Curriculum, Part II

by Mario McKenna, M.S.

Photographs courtesy of Mario McKenna.

三十六 Sanseru Kata

If you were to ask a Nahate student what is one of the most notable techniques of Sanseru, he would probably answer that it is the use of the elbow. The elbow strike is referred to as *enpiuchi* or *hijiate* in Japanese, and is a powerful technique in the old karate (Okinawan: *toudi*) arsenal. Compared to the fist, the elbow is much stronger, larger, and closer to the body, which allows it to concentrate more energy into a strike. It also requires less impact training (e.g., makiwara) compared to the fist, and is less prone to injury. Perhaps a better saying than the traditional karate maxim of "One punch, one kill" would be "One elbow, one kill." Before examining the elbow strike and other techniques in Sanseru, let's review a little bit of Sanseru's and its different versions.

Odd Man Out

Sanseru is the odd man out in Nahate katas. Compared to the other main Nahate katas, it seems like a kata with multiple personalities. When we examine the Higaonna Kanryo (1850–1915) lineage of Sanseru, we can see three main versions:[1]

1) Miyagi Chojun (宮城 長順 1888–1952) version,
2) Kyoda Juhatsu (許田 重発 1887–1968) version, and
3) Higa Seko (比嘉 世幸 1898–1966) version.

I must admit my bias at this point and feel that the Kyoda version is probably the closest to the original that Higaonna taught. There is enough anecdotal evidence to argue for this. There are stories of Miyagi's being upset when he returned from his military duty to find out that Kyoda had learned Sanseru; Kyoda's being noted as an expert in this kata and performing it at many festivals and demonstrations; Miyagi's deferring to Kyoda with respect to Sanseru kata among his students; the presence of the midlevel block, front kick, and elbow strike—which are signature techniques of Miyagi found in his version of Sanseru—and Miyagi katas Gekisai I and II; and the statement from Miyagi Kei (1919–2009) (Miyagi Chojun's son) that his father learned this kata from Kyoda. Ironically, however, compared to the Kyoda, the Miyagi version is now the most common version taught in the majority of Goju-Ryu dojos around the world.

The Higa version of Sanseru is a bit of a conundrum in that it seems to mix the Miyagi and Kyoda versions. We shouldn't really be surprised at this given the dual influence of Miyagi and Higaonna on Higa Seko.[2] This alone might be enough reason to explain the hybrid nature of the Higa Sanseru.[3] The Higa Sanseru has many techniques mixed from the Miyagi and Kyoda versions, as well as its own unique techniques. For example, like the Kyoda version, there is a knee strike in place of the double kick at the beginning. Like the Miyagi version, it uses the midlevel block, front kick, and elbow combination. And uniquely it turns in the opposite direction when performing the final crane posture.

[1] Though historically important, we will limit our discussion to the Higaonna Sanseru kata and exclude the Uechi-Ryu-version of the same kata.
[2] See http://en.wikipedia.org/wiki/Seko_Higa.
[3] As an aside, many of Higa Seko's students know and teach the Miyagi version of Sanseru, as well as the Higa version of the same kata. More recently, the main Higa lineage group, the International Karatedo Kobudo Federation, emphasizes the Miyagi version to more freely interact with other Goju-Ryu associations and events with respect to kata.

Escape Technique and Joint Lock

Like Sanchin and Sesan earlier, Sanseru kata begins with three steps in Sanchin stance in combination with three reverse punches and three midlevel blocks. The first major technique after this sequence is an escape and joint lock technique akin to the aikijujutsu wristlock (*nikkajo*), although there are some differences in how the technique is performed in the Kyoda, Miyagi, and Higa versions. The seized wrist is used to secure the opponent's hand, while the other hand locks the opponent's elbow. The opponent's balance is broken by stepping back into a forward stance, which also provides additional leverage.

2) Sanseru To'on escape and lock, and applied.

1) Sanseru Goju escape and lock, and applied.

Elbow Strike, Hook Punch, and Low Side Kick

Sanseru introduces the vertical elbow strike in conjunction with a forward stance. The forward stance deserves a bit of discussion at this point. One of the first things we should notice is that the forward stance appears often in the Sanseru kata, is absent in the Sanchin kata, and only appears once in the Sesan kata. We should stop and ask ourselves why that is. As we saw earlier in the opening segment of Sanseru, the forward stance provides greater leverage and the ability to break the opponent's balance when we execute the escape and joint lock technique. However, there is much more to the forward stance than this. In Sanseru, the forward stance is used as a means of moving quickly forward to enter and occupy an opponent's space, and to transfer body weight into the strike. When this is combined with the use of the vertical elbow, the result is a technique that can crush an opponent.

At this point we should note that there are substantial differences among the three versions with respect to the techniques performed before the vertical elbow strike. In the Higa and Miyagi versions, a midlevel block and front kick are performed in Sanchin stance, while in the Kyoda version, an inverted rising block in Sesan stance is performed with no kick. These are very important differences that need to be considered when examining the evolution of Sanseru kata—or any Nahate kata, for that matter. It provides a sort of a DNA signature, if you will. At any rate, this difference in the stances and techniques performed prior to the execution of the vertical elbow strike is important, as it changes the dynamics and functionality of the technique quite drastically. The Kyoda version teaches much more clearly the importance of entering straight into a technique (*irimi*).

Following the vertical elbow strike, a left punch is delivered. Here there are some minor variations, with the Higa and Kyoda versions remaining in a half-facing (*hanmi*) forward stance before delivering the punch, while the Miyagi version squares the waist and performs the punch. Functionally the technique is the same in all the versions and is typically used as a quick follow-up strike to the elbow strike.

The final portion of this sequence is the low side kick, and here we can see differences among the different versions. In the Miyagi and Higa versions, the leg is drawn back slowly, then the kick is delivered quickly, and then retracted quickly and placed on the ground. In the Kyoda version, the leg is pulled back rapidly, the kick delivered quickly, but the leg is left extended, and then placed on the ground. Regardless of how the technique is performed, there are many interesting uses for the low side kick. At a superficial level, much like Sesan earlier, the kick can be delivered directly to the knee with very dangerous consequences. However, as I discussed in the Sesan portion, there are many other interesting uses for this technique, some of which include throws and sweeps, and Sanseru introduces a new perspective on how to use them.

Sanseru Goju-ryu elbow sequence and application.

2a–d) Sanseru Tou'on-ryu
elbow sequence and application.

1a
Sanseru
elbow
sequence
variation
applied.

1b

1c

2a
Sanseru
Goju-ryu
Tou'on-ryu
low side kick.

2b Applied.

Low Cross Block

The next portion of the kata has the performer execute two separate low cross blocks in succession: one with open hands and one with fists, in a horse stance. The sequence in the Miyagi and Higa versions is with an open-hand block first, followed by a fist block, while in the Kyoda version, the sequence is reversed. Regardless of the sequence of open to closed block or vice versa, the low cross block is an interesting technique. On the surface this technique could be interpreted literally as a low block, perhaps against a kick, but, as I stated previously, form does not always follow function. Of course with a little experimentation it is also soon apparent that this is a very superficial and potentially dangerous technique to use by the defender. Instead we should remember that karate has many jujutsu-like applications found in its katas, and a key concept is the use of entangling techniques (karamidi). This gives us a clue to decipher its meaning. For example, in the Kyoda version of Sanseru, this section of the kata is taught as a joint lock and rotary throw, somewhat similar to aikido's rotary throw (kaiten nage).

Right: Sanseru X-blocks

Below: Sanseru X-block sequences. 1a-c: Sanseru Goju-ryu. 2a-c: Sanseru Tou'on-ryu.

Double Block and Double Punch

The next technique that we will look at is the double block and double punch combination found near the end of Sanseru. Here again the three versions of Sanseru differ in their execution of the technique, with the Miyagi version transitioning from a horse stance to a Sanchin stance, the Higa version transitioning from a rooted stance to a natural stance, and the Kyoda version transitioning from a cat stance to a forward stance. The differences in stances are important because they dictate the position of the hands in the double block. In the Miyagi version, which uses a horse stance, the hips are turned in, and therefore the arms are held close to the body. In contrast, the Higa and Kyoda versions use a natural stance and a forward stance so the hips are turned out, and therefore the arms are extended. This changes the function of the technique somewhat, but at its heart it is a technique for seizing control of the opponent.

1a
Sanseru
Goju-ryu
double
block.

1b
Applied.

2a

Sanseru
Goju-ryu
double
block.

2b
Applied.

The double block is followed by a double punch, which is a new technique and was not found in the Sanchin or Sesan kata. Interestingly the double punch is also a technique rarely found in Japanese jujutsu, and we can say that it is unique to karate (Hirakami, 2000). There are various applications based on different instructors' teachings, the most rudimentary of which is to use this technique to deflect an opponent's attack and simultaneously strike the body. Of course, there are more interesting and dangerous techniques, especially when linked to the previous double block technique and the entangling technique concept (karamidi) is incorporated into it.

Sanseru Tou'on-ryu double blocks and applications.

Crane Posture

At the end of Sanseru the performer executes the crane posture. This posture consists of one arm extended and the other held close to the body with the wrists of both hands bent and the fingers bunched together. In Sanseru, the crane posture is performed with a turning movement, with the performer finishing in a horse stance. Here again the three versions of Sanseru differ in the direction and the number of degrees they turn. The Miyagi version turns approximately 220° to the right, the Higa version turns to the left approximately 50°, and the Kyoda version turns 90° to the right. The direction and number of degrees of the turn are important, as they dictate the angle and direction of entry. However, if we apply the entangling principle (karamidi), we can see that one use of this technique is to lock the opponent's arm and drop him to the ground.

With the progression from Sanchin to Sesan, and now to Sanseru, an interesting observation begins to emerge. All three Nahate katas begin with the fundamental midlevel deflection, and punch from Sanchin stance repeated three times, then introduce an escape technique, followed by a new impact technique, before then finishing with a grappling technique—a pedagogically sound progression.

There is a reason this final posture is referred to as the crane posture, much like why a circle block is sometimes referred to as "tiger mouth" (tora guchi), but to explain this might be giving too much away. So I will leave it up to the readers to ponder this by themselves, but not without providing a hint. Sanchin and Sesan katas end with the tiger-mouth posture, while Sanseru and Suparimpei end with the crane posture (tsuru no kamae). In other words, the tiger and the crane combine to create a synergy of karate techniques. This is expressed in the Chinese idiom, "Like a tiger growing wings" (Hirakami, 2000).

Sanseru
Goju
crane
posture.

1a

1b

Applied.

2a
Sanseru
Tou'on-ryu
crane
posture.

2b   Applied.

壱百歩連   BECHURIN / PECHURIN • SUPAREMPEI   壱百零八

After learning the Sanchin, Sesan, and Sanseru katas and coming to an understanding of their techniques, we arrive at the final kata to be learned. But what do we call it? In Goju-Ryu it is typically referred to as Suparimpei (and occasionally Pechurin Jo), while in Tou'on-Ryu it is called Bechurin or Pechurin (both pronunciations are considered acceptable). There has been much theorizing as to the origin of the names and with respect to which name is correct, but this is beyond the scope of this essay. For those interested in this topic, I would recommend reading the work of Kinjo Akio and Tokashiki Iken. Both researchers present some excellent historical and linguistic research into its possible origins. That said, for the remainder of this part of the series I will use the name Suparimpei to refer to the kata used in Goju-Ryu, and Bechurin as the kata used in Tou'on-Ryu.

In traditional dojos, from the time a person learns Sanchin to the time he or she learns Suparimpei, it is a very long apprenticeship. But nowadays we see junior high school children performing this kata at regional, national, or international competitions, on DVDs by different instructors, or on the internet, where we are subjected to varying levels of competence. Regardless of the medium, I am inclined to think, as Hirakami Nobuyuki stated, that you cannot help but feel a bit sad because the sense of appreciation toward the opportunity to learn this kata is all but gone (Hirakami, 2000).

Double Palm Strike to the Sides

Like the katas learned before, both Bechurin and Suparimpei use the same base techniques for their opening sequence: advancing three times in Sanchin stance along with three reverse punches and three midlevel blocks. From here the palms are brought in front of the chest and then extended to the right and left in a slow and deliberate manner. In Suparimpei there is a distinct lowering and rising of the body when performing this technique, which is absent from Tou'on-Ryu. In addition, Tou'on-Ryu uses a thumb strike identical to the one used in Uechi-Ryu in place of the palm strike found in Goju-Ryu.

An application for this technique is an escape from a double hand grab that simultaneously pulls the opponent and positions him for the next technique. Tou'on-Ryu's use of the thumb strike opens up some different applications, especially when we consider the attacker trying to grab hold of you. In Tou'on-Ryu the power of the thumb strike is passed down through the story of Yabu Kentsu (1866–1937). In their version of the story, during his military days as a sergeant in the Japanese army, Yabu faced court martial for striking and severely injuring a superior officer. An inquiry exonerated him, since Yabu apparently only used his palm to strike the man. However in Tou'on-Ryu the damage inflicted was the result of a well-placed thumb strike.

Suparempei
Bechurin
Goju-ryu
Tou'on-ryu right and left palm strikes.

Suparempei double palm strike applied.

Bechurin double palm strike applied.

Bechurin Tou'on'ryu thumb stirke.

Circle Block, Hooking Block, and Sword-Hand Strike

Following the double palm strike, two circle blocks are performed while moving forward. These are followed by a hooking block and a sword-hand strike. There are some minor differences here between Suparimpei and Bechurin in how the hooking block and sword-hand strike are performed, but the techniques are essentially analogous. Both sets of techniques are repeated to the four compass points. As I mentioned earlier, the circle block has many jujutsu-like applications contained within it. As most of us know, trying to apply any sort of locking technique on a resisting opponent can be very difficult. Performing the circle block twice is one way of overcoming an opponent's resistance by reversing direction and collapsing the opponent backward with an entering throw akin to aikido's *iriminage*, Tenjin Shinryo-ryu jujutsu's *tengusho*, or Shotokan's *kubiwa*. Using two circle blocks in succession is akin to saying that the tiger bites twice (Hirakami, 2000).

Suparempei:
1a) circle block,
1b) hook block,
1c) fingertip strike.

Bechurin:
2a) circle block,
2b) hook block,
2c) sword hand strike

After the two circle blocks comes the hooking block and sword-hand strike sequence. There are many different explanations for this technique depending on the teacher and the respective school, but the superficial explanation is to parry, seize an attacker's arm, and to follow up with a strike of your own to the torso. Of course, there is nothing wrong with this explanation, but there are other, more dangerous uses of it. A simple variation would be to hook the head and use the sword-hand to strike the neck.

Left: Suparempei
Bechurin
circle block
applied.

Right: Suparempei
Bechurin
finger tip
strike
applied.

Circle Block/Backhand Block

The next sequence differs quite markedly between Bechurin and Suparimpei. In Suparimpei there is a series of three circle blocks performed in a cat stance, a pairing of techniques that we have encountered before in the Sesan kata. In Tou'on-Ryu we find the use of a backhand block (*ura uke*) performed in a high cat stance. We know from our earlier discussion of Sesan when the cat stance and circle block were introduced, the intention was to entangle an attacker's arms and then drop him to the ground, but since Tou'on-Ryu does not use a circle block in this part of the kata, what is the purpose of the backhand block? The answer may lie in an old anecdote provided by the late Matsubayashi-Ryu founder Nagamine Shoshin's book. Nagamine (1986: 100) describes a technique used in an altercation that involved Higaonna Kanryo. The original Japanese translation reads as follows:

Kanryo quickly slid back as the punch came towards him and at
the same time used his right wrist to strike the man's forearm down.[4]

The reference to using the wrist suggests that Higaonna used a backhand block to
defend himself. This is the same application that is taught in Tou'on-Ryu for this
portion of Bechurin kata. Essentially the technique is used to either strike or to
seize the limb of the attacker in a fast, whipping action.

1a) Suparempei cat stance and circle block.
1b) Bechurin cat stance and back hand block.
1c) Bechurin back of hand block applied.

Entering the Gate

An important characteristic of both Bechurin and Suparimpei is the use of
the eight gates or directions. In Sanchin kata the student learns to execute techniques toward the east and west. In Sesan and Sanseru karate this is expanded
and students repeat techniques to the four cardinal points of east, west, south,
and north.[5] These are expanded upon in the last Nahate kata to include an additional four points on a diagonal plane, so that now techniques are performed to all
eight compass points. There are two main reasons for the introduction of these
additional four points in Bechurin and Suparimpei. The first is that it brings a very
strong sense of spatial awareness that teaches the performer to let loose techniques
at will in any direction. The second is that karate is a method of self-protection and
as such it is necessary to be able to receive an attack from any direction. Therefore
Bechurin and Suparimpei teach the student these concepts in a systematic way.

[4] This translation was done by the author of this article, Mario McKenna.
[5] Traditionally, katas were started facing the east, and this direction is commonly noted in many earlier karate books from
the 1920s and 1930s.

Double Punch, Low Block, and Reverse Punch

The next sequence we'll look at is the double punch/low bock/reverse punch combination. Here again we see differences between Suparimpei and Bechurin in how these techniques are performed, but we can consider them analogous for the purpose of our discussion. In the previous kata, Sanseru, we saw the introduction of the double punch, but in Bechurin and Suparimpei we have the addition of the low block and reverse punch. The double punch is most often applied as a simultaneous block and counter. However, if we remember the principle of karamidi, then the double punch can entangle the opponent's arms, while the block can also be used to apply a joint lock followed by a reverse punch to finish the opponent. Indeed, there is an overt wrapping motion in the Tou'on-Ryu Bechurin kata that clearly shows this technique.

Below: Suparempei
double punch applied.

Right: Suparempei
double punch.

Above: Bechurin
double punch.

1a

Bechurin
double punch
applied.

1b

1c

Uppercut, One-Knuckle Thrust, or Single-Finger Thrust, and Double Low Block

The next sequence also differs between Bechurin and Suparimpei. In Bechurin the performer takes a double guard position with the arms and stands in a forward stance. In this instance, the forward stance is unique in that the upper body is bent forward. In contrast, Suparimpei uses a horse stance and also assumes a double guard position, but the hands are held either in a one-knuckle fist or a single-finger hand.[6] The one-knuckle fist is formed by protruding the first joint of the index finger and supporting it with the thumb. The single-finger hand is formed by extending the index finger, bending the remaining fingers at the first joint, and tightly squeezing the fingers together.

From these respective stances and hand postures, both katas deliver strikes, but again there is an apparent difference in the target area. In Bechurin the uppercut is directed toward the head. Suparimpei, on the other hand, appears to direct its strike to the torso from a horse stance. This is a very interesting difference and somewhat paradoxical. Both the one-knuckle fist and the single-finger hand lack strength in directly attacking the torso, but are excellent tools for attacking the face or other vital points. Yet only Bechurin overtly attacks the face. This is something I would ask the reader to consider.

Suparempei Higa double guard.

Suparempei Higa hand strike.

Suparempei Miyagi double guard.

Suparempei Miyagi hand strike.

Bechurin double guard.

Bechurin upper cut.

The next movement in both Bechurin and Suparimpei involves dropping down into a horse stance and executing a double low block. At face value, this technique is a little difficult to understand, but if we remember that entangling, seizing, and locking techniques are part of all the Nahate katas, then we can work out the meaning of this technique. This would imply that the initial double guard position is used to grab or entangle the attacker's arm, and then stepping through to strike redoubles its power. This also allows the defender to transition into the horse stance, where the double low block makes more sense. A simple example would be to use the double low block to not only apply a joint lock, but also to use it as a hammer strike.

1a) Bechurin double guard applied.
1b) Suparempei double guard applied.

1c) Suparempei Bechurin double low block.
1d) Suparempei Bechurin double low block applied.

---

[6] The single-finger hand is also called the "blade of grass" hand and is illustrated in the *Bubishi*. This hand formation is more commonly found in the Higa lineage of Suparimpei.

113

Divergence

After the double low block, there is a divergence in the techniques performed between Suparimpei and Bechurin. Bechurin lacks the pressing block, front kick, horizontal elbow strike, backfist strike, and hand escape; the follow-up elbow strike, backfist strike; and the final finger-tip strike before the crane posture.[7] Therefore, for the remaining part of this discussion I will focus on the techniques common in both katas.

Crescent Kick

The crescent kick in Suparimpei is preceded by a 360° turn, whereas in Bechurin it is preceded by an 180° turn. The kick in both katas is performed at head height, with the right leg into the palm of the left hand. This technique is commonly seen as a wrist escape in Goju-Ryu, or as a kick to the opponent's face in both Tou'on-Ryu and Goju-Ryu. In Tou'on-Ryu the crescent kick is also sometimes applied as a flying kick followed by a low sweep, similar to some Northern Chinese gongfu systems. Regardless, these are surface-level applications and not very satisfying. When examining this technique, it is vital to remember that karate is a method of self-protection and applications must be applied in this context.

Suparempei
Bechurin
crescent kick.

[7] As an aside, this is one possible explanation that I would put forward regarding the difference in names between Suparimpei and Bechurin.

114

Suparempei
double kick.

Bechurin
double kick.

Double Kick

Immediately after the crescent kick, a double kick is performed in both katas. In Suparimpei this takes the form of two consecutive snapping front kicks delivered after jumping vertically. The Tou'on-Ryu method is quite different in that the performer also leaps vertically, but the kick is executed with the legs straight, giving the outward appearance of a vertical scissor kick. Each of these methods has its own unique applications, but at a rudimentary level the double kick is used to finish an attacker after controlling his body. For the Suparimpei

Suparempei
Bechurin
double kick
applied.

kata, one of the more interesting applications that I learned from Tokashiki Iken (founder of the Goju-Ryu Tomarite Association) could be described as a bando-style knee strike, in which you place one foot on the opponent's hip and use it to launch a knee strike with the other leg to the head.

115

Suparempei crane posture.

Suparempei crane posture applied.

Bechurin crane posture.

Bechurin crane posture applied.

Crane Posture

As with Sanseru, this is the final combative posture, and here also differences emerge between Suparimpei and Bechurin. In Suparimpei the performer does not spin as much compared to Sanseru, but still ends in a horse stance. There are also some minor intergroup differences between the Miyagi and Higa versions, with the hands forming the crane posture traveling from high to middle in the Higa version and from low to middle in the Miyagi version. In Bechurin there is no turning at all, and the performer simply steps back and assumes the crane posture with the hands. But interestingly this is immediately followed by a hooking block. This difference may be the result of the *kuden* (spoken lessons) handed down in Tou'on-Ryu, which says that the final combative posture of any kata is not fixed once the kata is learned and understood. As we have already discussed the crane posture and its use in the section on Sanseru kata, I will not explain it here, but would

Bechurin
crane posture
applied.

encourage the reader to think about her own applications—especially when applying the principle of *tuidi* (grappling), karamidi (entangling), *chugedi* (locking), and other ideas that have been introduced in this article.

Bibliography

Hirakami, N. (2001). Koden Ryukyu kenpo: Nahate no himitsu (The ancient transmission of Ryukyu boxing: The secret of Nahate). *Gekkan Hiden* ([*Martial*] *Secrets Monthly*): Issues 1–10.

Kinjo, A. (1999). *Karate denshin roku (A true record of the transmission of karate)*. Okinawa: Tosho Center.

Nagamine, S. (1986). *Okinawa karate sumo meijin-den (Tales of Okinawa's karate and sumo masters)*. Tokyo: Ouraisha.

Tokashiki, I. (1991). *Gohaku-kai nenkanshi (Gohaku-kai yearbook)*, Vol. 4. Naha: Published privately.

Acknowledgments

I would like to extend my sincerest thanks to Mr. Maik Hassel for taking the photographs that illustrate this article, and to Mr. Olivier Riche for posing for the photographs.

index

Made in the USA
San Bernardino, CA
23 November 2015